# Contents

**On the Front Cover:**
Orange Stir Fry, pg. 58
Double Chocolate Chip Cookies, pg. 41
Beefy Mushroom Salisbury Steak, pg. 5
Cauliflower Crust Pizza, pg. 83
Cornbread Biscuits, pg. 26

**On the Back Cover:**
Bruschetta Chicken, pg. 67
Caramel Apple Pie, pg. 38
Rhubarb BBQ Sauce, pg. 50
Gingerbread, pg. 28
Balsamic Braised Red Cabbage, pg. 89

*For More Fun Stuff, Go To: www.JanevasIdealRecipes.com*

# Beef & Pork Main Dishes

**TIP:** When you are at the grocer, an easy rule to find lean beef quickly is that anything with "round," "chuck" or "loin" in its name is usually either extra lean or lean. Round and chuck steaks are often tougher cuts -- use an acidic marinade to tenderize the meat for at least an hour before cooking; these cuts also do well in crockpot recipes. A combination of lemon juice, light soy sauce and minced garlic, for example, tenderizes meat quickly. Do not add oil to your marinades as this introduces unnecessary fat.

**Italian Sausage Meatloaf**
Page 7

**Pizza Burger Casserole**
Page 8

**Sausage Zucchini Lasagna**
Page 12

**Crack Slaw**
Page 6

**Cinnamon Apple Pork Tenderloin**
*Crockpot Recipe*
Page 10

**Pork Carnitas**
*Crockpot Recipe*
Page 11

*www.JanevasIdealRecipes.com*

# Beef Recipes

## BBQ SLOPPY JOES

**Ingredients:**
16 oz. lean ground beef
½ C. chopped green onion
½ C. chopped green bell pepper
2 tsp. onion powder
2 tsp. salt
1 C. canned diced tomatoes w/juice (no added sugar)
½ C. Walden Farms honey BBQ sauce
1 tsp. lemon juice
1 tsp. white vinegar
1 tsp. yellow mustard

**Directions:**
1. In a large fry pan over medium/medium high heat, brown hamburger. Halfway through browning add green onion, green pepper, onion powder and salt. Drain any fat.
2. Meanwhile pour tomatoes into a blender; blend well.
3. Add blended tomatoes and all remaining ingredients to the meat mixture. Heat till bubbling; turn down heat and simmer 25 minutes, stirring occasionally.

**Servings:** Entire recipe = 16 oz. lean protein + 2 C. veggies; ½ recipe = 8 oz. lean protein + 1 C. veggies

**Tip:** Serve BBQ Sloppy Joes on the Potato Pancake Buns, pg. 31; add

1 unrestricted to the servings, if consuming.

## BEEFY MUSHROOM SALISBURY STEAK

**Ingredients:** (Salisbury steak)
16 oz. lean ground beef
3 T. liquid egg whites
½ tsp. soy sauce
3 tsp. Dijon mustard
2 T. Walden Farms ketchup

**Ingredients:** (mushrooms)
1 ¾ C. sliced fresh mushrooms (I like maitake mushrooms)
¼ C. sliced green onions
2 tsp. olive oil
2 T. soy sauce
1 T. water

**Directions:**
1. In a large bowl, add all ingredients for the Salisbury steak; mix with hands.
2. Form 4 equal oval patties; set aside.
3. In a medium fry pan, heat olive oil over medium high heat. Add all mushroom ingredients and stir fry until mushrooms are lightly browned and green onions slightly limp. Remove from pan and place on a covered plate to keep warm.
4. In the same frying pan, cook Salisbury steaks about 3 minutes each side over medium/medium high heat or until done.
5. Plate Salisbury steaks; top with mushroom mixture.

**Servings:** Entire recipe = 16 oz. lean protein + 2 C. veggies; ½ recipe = 8 oz. lean protein + 1 C. veggies

**TIP:** Excellent served over Cauliflower Mashed Faux-tatoes, pg. 90.

## BETTER THAN TAKE-OUT BEEF & BROCCOLI STIR FRY

**Ingredients:**
16 oz. lean beef, sliced in stir fry strips (round steak, tenderloin, etc.)
2 C. broccoli slaw or florets
1 C. shredded cabbage
1 C. sliced fresh mushrooms
4 T. soy sauce
4 T. Walden Farms honey Dijon dressing
2 T. Walden Farms pancake syrup
Garlic powder, to taste
Onion powder, to taste
IP salt, to taste
Black pepper, to taste
2 tsp. olive oil
Cooking spray

**Directions:**
1. Preheat oven to 425 degrees.
2. Place the broccoli and cabbage in a resealable bag with the olive oil and garlic powder. Shake to coat.
3. Transfer to a baking sheet and spread out. Roast 15 - 20 minutes, stirring once during roasting.
4. Meanwhile, heat a skillet over medium/medium high heat. Spray coat with cooking spray; stir fry the mushrooms 10 minutes. Sprinkle with onion powder as you cook.

Add salt and pepper, to taste. (If the pan gets too dry you may add fat free chicken broth a splash at a time to help cook the mushrooms.)

5. Add beef strips and continue to stir fry until beef is browned.

6. Add roasted vegetables, soy sauce, honey Dijon dressing and syrup. Stir fry until heated through.

**Servings:** Entire recipe = 16 oz. lean protein + 4 C. veggies; ½ recipe = 8 oz. lean protein + 2 C. veggies

## BIG MACK MEATLOAF

**Ingredients:**
14 oz. lean ground beef
1 egg, slightly beaten
1/3 C. chopped pickles (sugar free)
1 T. Walden Farms ketchup
1 T. Dijon mustard
½ tsp. IP salt
¼ tsp. black pepper
1 tsp. onion powder
2/3 C. chopped yellow onions, raw
Walden Farms thousand island dressing, to taste
Cooking spray

**Directions:**
1. Preheat oven to 350 degrees.
2. Mix together all ingredients except raw onions and thousand island dressing.
3. Press into 2 sprayed mini loaf pans, 5 ¾" x 3" x 2 1/8". Bake 25 - 30 minutes.
4. Serve topped with raw onions and Walden Farms thousand island dressing.

**Servings:** Entire recipe = 16 oz. lean protein (14 oz. lean ground beef + 2 oz. whole egg) + 1 C. veggies; ½ recipe = 8 oz. lean protein + ½ C. veggies.

**TIP:** This meatloaf is delicious served over Cauliflower Mashed Faux-tatoes, pg. 90.

## CRACK SLAW

**Ingredients:**
16 oz. ground beef
1 T. + 1 tsp. olive oil
1 tsp. minced garlic
3 ½ C. shredded cabbage
½ C. chopped green onion
Salt and pepper to taste

**Sauce:**
½ tsp. sugar free sweetener, granulated
¼ tsp. ground ginger (powder)
1 tsp. white vinegar
2 T. soy sauce
½ tsp. chili powder (or hot sauce)

**Directions:**
1. In a large skillet, combine minced garlic with ground beef and brown over medium/medium high heat. Season with salt and pepper, to taste.
2. Meanwhile, combine all the ingredients for the sauce in a small bowl; mix.
3. Drain any fat from the ground beef and discard, remove beef from pan and set aside.
4. In the same skillet heat the olive oil over medium/medium high heat; add the green onion and cabbage. Stir fry until cabbage is slightly wilted and tender.
5. Stir in the sauce and add the meat; stir to combine. Serve hot.

**Servings:** Entire recipe = 16 oz. lean protein + 4 C. veggies; ½ recipe = 8 oz. lean protein + 2 C. veggies.

## DIRTY RICE

**Ingredients:**
16 oz. lean ground beef
2 T. Sausage Seasoning, pg. 51
1 tsp. Cajun seasoning
¼ tsp. rubbed sage
4 tsp. olive oil
2/3 C. diced green pepper
½ C. diced celery
1 tsp. minced garlic
1/3 C. chopped green onion
2 ½ C. cauliflower florets, riced

**Directions:**
1. Place ground beef in a large frying pan. Sprinkle with sausage, Cajun and sage seasonings; brown over medium/medium high heat. Set aside when browned and keep warm over low heat.
2. Meanwhile, heat olive oil in a medium frying pan over medium/medium high heat. Add green pepper, celery and garlic; stir fry 4 minutes. Add green onion; stir fry another 4 minutes.
3. Add riced cauliflower, lower heat to medium, cover and cook another 6 minutes.
4. Add cauliflower mixture to ground beef mixture and heat through; serve.

**Servings:** Entire recipe = 16 oz. lean protein + 4 C. veggies; ½ recipe = 8 oz. lean protein + 2 C. veggies

## FIESTA BEEF NACHOS

*Individual sweet peppers take the place of tortilla chips. Great finger food.*

**Ingredients:**
1 ½ C. (approximately 10) mini sweet peppers, assorted colors
6 oz. lean ground turkey or beef
2 - 3 tsp. Taco Seasoning, pg. 52
¼ C. chopped fresh mushrooms
¼ C. chopped green onions
1 large egg, slightly beaten
Olive oil spray

**Directions:**
1. Preheat oven to 425 degrees.
2. Prepare sweet peppers by cutting off tops and cutting in half lengthwise. Clean out membrane and seeds.
3. Spray mist olive oil on a baking sheet; transfer peppers to baking sheet cut side up. Spray mist the peppers lightly with olive oil. Roast 10 - 12 minutes.
4. When finished roasting, remove from oven and set pan aside. Turn oven temperature down to 350 degrees.
5. Meanwhile, preheat a skillet over medium/medium high heat. Add ground turkey or beef, taco seasoning, mushrooms and green onions. Brown meat and vegetables together, stirring to cook through. Drain off any fat; set meat mixture

aside and cool.
6. In a small bowl, lightly beat one large egg. Pour into cooled meat mixture; mix.
7. Fill the pepper halves with the meat mixture, stuffing them as neatly as possible.
8. Bake 15 minutes. Sprinkle with more taco seasoning and/or salt before serving.

**Servings:** 8 oz. lean protein (6 oz. lean beef + 2 oz. whole egg) + 2 C. veggies

## FRENCH DIP AU JUS

*Crockpot recipe*

**Ingredients:**
2 lb. chuck roast
¼ C. soy sauce
2 C. fat free beef broth
1 T. Dijon mustard
2 tsp. onion powder
1 tsp. IP salt
1 tsp. black pepper
1 tsp. minced garlic

**Directions:**
1. Place all ingredients in the crockpot except roast; stir to mix.
2. Trim any fat from roast and add to crockpot. Cover and cook on low 7 - 8 hours.

**Servings:** Entire recipe = 32 oz. lean protein; ¼ recipe = 8 oz. lean protein

## ITALIAN SAUSAGE MEATLOAF

*Makes two mini loaves*

**Ingredients:**
16 oz. lean ground beef (or chicken or turkey)
2 T. Sausage Seasoning, pg. 51
6 T. Spaghizza Sauce, pg. 51 (divided)
1 C. shredded zucchini
1/3 C. liquid egg whites
Cooking spray

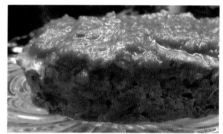

**Directions:**
1. Preheat oven to 350 degrees.
2. In a small bowl, microwave zucchini 1 minute. Blot with paper towels to absorb excess moisture; set aside to cool.
3. In a medium bowl, mix ground beef with Sausage Seasoning; set aside.
4. In a separate medium bowl, whisk egg whites, 2 T. of the Spaghizza Sauce, and cooled zucchini. Add to meat mixture and mix till incorporated.
5. Spray two 5 3/8" x 3" x 2 1/8" mini loaf pans; divide meat mixture in half and place each half in separate loaf pans, pressing down firmly and evenly.
6. Bake 25 minutes; remove meatloaves from pans; plate meatloaves.
7. Heat the remaining Spaghizza Sauce (4 T.) and spread over loaves; serve.

**Servings:** 2 meatloaves = 16 oz. lean protein + 1 ½ C. veggies; 1 meatloaf = 8 oz. lean protein + ¾ C. veggies

## NAKED BURRITO CASSEROLE

Ingredients:
8 oz. lean ground beef (or chicken or turkey)
2-3 tsp. Taco Seasoning, pg. 52
10 oz. can mild diced tomatoes & green chiles
4 eggs + 2 egg whites, slightly beaten
Fresh cilantro, chopped (to taste)
*Mockamole, pg. 50; optional
Shredded lettuce, unlimited
*Pico de Gallo, pg. 50; optional
Cooking spray

Directions:
1.  Preheat oven to 400 degrees.
2.  In a medium frying pan, brown ground beef seasoned with taco seasoning.
3.  Spread ground beef evenly in a sprayed 9 x 9 inch baking dish.
4.  Drain canned tomatoes & chiles; spread evenly over beef mixture.
5.  Pour beaten eggs over the top; sprinkle with chopped cilantro (to taste).
6.  Bake 25 minutes or just until center of casserole is set and eggs no longer jiggle.  Do not over bake, or eggs will go from tender to tough.
7.  Cut casserole into 4 squares. Using 2 squares, stack one on top of the other on a plate and serve topped with shredded lettuce, cilantro, Mockamole and Pico de Gallo Salsa.

8.  Refrigerate the remaining 2 squares for another serving.

Servings:  Entire recipe = 16 oz. lean protein + 2 C. veggies; ½ recipe = 8 oz. lean protein + 1 C. veggies

TIP:  *If adding Mockamole and/or Pico De Gallo to the dish, measure and add to the veggie count.

## PERFECT STEAK

Ingredients:
1 - 8 oz. lean steak
Garlic powder, to taste
Salt and pepper, to taste

Directions:
1.  Preheat oven to 500 degrees.
2.  Season steak with garlic powder, salt and pepper.  Sear steak in a hot skillet or grill pan on medium high heat for 30 seconds on each side.
3.  Place steak in baking pan and put in preheated oven.
4.  For a one inch thick steak, roast for 3 minutes, turn over and roast another 3 minutes for medium doneness.
5. Plate steak; let rest 6-8 minutes before eating.

Servings: 8 oz. lean protein

## PIZZA BURGER CASSEROLE
*You will need to make the Spaghizza Sauce recipe as part of this dish*

Ingredients:
8  oz. lean ground beef
4  eggs + 2 egg whites
1 ¾ C. shredded zucchini
1  C. Spaghizza Sauce, pg. 51
½  C. chopped bell peppers  (I use green and yellow)

½  C. sliced mushrooms
¼  C. sliced green onions
Onion powder, to taste
Garlic powder, to taste
Salt and pepper, to taste
Cooking spray

Directions:
1.  Preheat oven to 400 degrees.
2.  Place shredded zucchini in a strainer, sprinkle on about ½ tsp. salt and mix; set aside.
3.  In a medium sized fry pan over medium/medium high heat, brown ground beef.  Season with onion powder, garlic powder, salt and pepper, to taste.  Halfway through browning the ground beef, add bell peppers, mushrooms and green onions.  Stir to cook veggies and finish browning the ground beef. Drain any fat.  Set aside.
4.  In a medium bowl, place the 4 eggs and 2 egg whites; using a whisk, slightly beat eggs together until mixed.  Set aside.
5.  Place the shredded zucchini on a work surface.  Press with several paper towels to absorb the moisture out of the zucchini, then put into the egg mixture and stir to incorporate evenly.
6.  Spray a 9 x 9 inch baking dish with cooking spray.
7.  Evenly layer the ground beef mixture, then the spaghizza sauce and  top with the egg mixture.  Season with salt and pepper.
8.  Bake 25 minutes or just until center of casserole is set and eggs no longer jiggle.  Do not over bake, or eggs will go from tender to tough.

Servings:  Entire recipe = 16 oz. lean protein + 4 C. veggies; ½ recipe = 8 oz. lean protein + 2 C. veggies

TIP:  *Make the Spaghizza sauce ahead and refrigerate or freeze for recipes like this.

## SHEPHERD'S PIE

**Ingredients:**
2 C. cauliflower florets
1 tsp. Walden Farms bacon dip, optional
1 egg
6 oz. BBQ Sloppy Joe recipe, pg. 5
(or 6 oz. seasoned ground beef)

**Directions:**
1. Make the Sloppy Joe recipe or brown 6 oz. seasoned ground beef (drain any fat).
2. Preheat oven to 350 degrees.
3. Boil the cauliflower florets until fork tender, 8 - 10 minutes. Drain and press with paper towels to absorb as much moisture as possible.
4. Place the cooked cauliflower, bacon dip (if using) and egg in a food processor; puree.
5. In an individual size casserole dish, place 6 oz. Sloppy Joe recipe (or seasoned ground beef). Layer cauliflower mixture on top; smooth with the back of a spoon to make it even.
6. Bake 30 minutes or until cauliflower mixture is set in the center.

**Servings:** 8 oz. lean protein (6 oz. ground beef + 2 oz. whole egg) + 2 C. veggies from cauliflower + ¾ C. veggies from Sloppy Joe mixture. If using the seasoned ground beef instead of the BBQ Sloppy Joe mixture, eliminate ¾ C. veggies from the serving size.

## STUFFED CHILE RELLENOS

**Ingredients:**
2 large Poblano chiles
14 oz. lean ground beef (or turkey or chicken)
1 C. cauliflower florets, riced
½ C. fresh mushrooms, chopped
2 T. chopped green onion
1 large egg, slightly beaten
Taco Seasoning (to taste), pg. 52
Spaghizza Sauce, pg. 51

**Directions:**
1. Make the Spaghizza Sauce recipe according to directions; set aside.
2. Preheat broiler. Line a baking sheet with aluminum foil and place the chiles on the baking sheet. Place under broiler as close as possible to heat by adjusting oven shelf to highest position.
3. Broil chiles until the skins are blackened and blistered.
4. Turn over and blacken the other side. This process takes about 10 - 15 minutes total. Do not over blacken or they will be mushy (still good but more challenging to work with).
5. When chiles are blackened, place them in a large resealable baggie while hot and seal the baggie. Let them sit in the baggie for about 20 minutes; this will make it easier to peel off the skin.
6. Heat oven to 350 degrees.
7. Meanwhile, brown the lean meat in a large frying pan on medium high heat and season with taco seasoning. Halfway through browning, add the mushrooms and green onion. Continue to cook until meat is browned. Drain any fat.
8. Add riced cauliflower to the meat mixture; stir fry for about one minute. Turn off heat and set mixture aside.
9. Chiles should be steamed and ready at this point. Take them out of the baggie and peel off as much of the blackened part as you can; it is not necessary to get all of it because skin can be eaten. Place chiles back on baking sheet.
10. With a knife, make a slit down the center from the top to the bottom part of the chile and scoop out the seeds with a spoon.
11. Spoon meat mixture evenly into each chile.
12. Slowly drizzle beaten egg over meat mixture of each stuffed chile, using a fork to move meat around slightly to get the egg down into the entire meat mixture.
13. Bake 10 - 15 minutes or until egg has cooked through.
14. Remove and top with ½ C. warmed Spaghizza Sauce and serve.

**Servings:** Entire recipe = 16 oz. lean protein (14 oz. lean meat + 2 oz. whole egg) + 4 C. veggies; ½ recipe= 8 oz. lean protein + 2 C. veggies.

## STUFFED GREEN PEPPERS CASSEROLE

**Ingredients:**
8 oz. lean ground beef (may use turkey or chicken)
2 C. cauliflower florets, riced
1 ¾ C. green bell peppers, cut in bite-size chunks (or you may use mixed colors)
¼ C. chopped green onion
1 tsp. olive oil
½ tsp. garlic powder
4 eggs + 2 egg whites
1 tsp. salt

1 tsp. lemon juice
1 tsp. onion powder
½ tsp. dry ground mustard
½ tsp. black pepper
Cooking spray

**Directions:**
1. Preheat oven to 425 degrees.
2. Place the bell pepper chunks into a large resealable bag with the olive oil and garlic powder. Shake to coat; spread out on a baking sheet. Roast in the oven for 15 minutes. After roasting, set aside. Turn oven down to 350 degrees.
3. Meanwhile, brown the ground beef and drain any fat. Season the meat while it is browning with your favorite seasonings (not listed as part of the recipe ingredients).
4. Prepare egg mixture by placing the eggs and egg whites in a medium bowl. Add the salt, lemon juice, onion powder, dry ground mustard and black pepper. Whisk until mixed; set aside.
5. Assemble the casserole by spraying an 8 x 8 inch casserole or baking dish with cooking spray. Place the browned meat in the dish, spreading evenly over the bottom.
6. Place the roasted bell peppers on top of the browned meat; layer the riced cauliflower on top of the peppers.
7. Pour the egg mixture evenly over the top of the casserole; sprinkle with chopped green onions. Bake 25 - 30 minutes or until eggs are set.

**Servings:** Entire recipe = 16 oz. lean protein (8 oz. ground meat + 4 whole eggs + 2 egg whites) + 4 C. veggies; ½ recipe = 8 oz. lean protein + 2 C. veggies.

**TIP:** Serve with sugar free hot sauce or buffalo hot sauce.

## SWEET AND SMOKY MEATBALLS
*Great dish for a potluck*

**Ingredients:** (meatballs)
1 lb + 12 oz. ground beef
2 eggs, slightly beaten
1 tsp. oregano
1 T. onion powder
1 tsp. rosemary
1 tsp. garlic powder
2 C. shredded zucchini
Salt & pepper, to taste

**Directions:**
1. Preheat oven to 350 degrees.
2. Place shredded zucchini in a medium microwave safe bowl; cook for 1 minute on high. Blot zucchini with paper towels to remove excess moisture.
3. Combine all ingredients well; form into meatballs.
4. Place meatballs on a baking sheet; bake 30 - 40 minutes or until meatballs are medium well to well done. Drain on paper towels.

**Ingredients:** (sauce)
½ C. Walden Farms cranberry spread
½ C. Walden Farms BBQ sauce, any flavor
¼ C. Walden Farms ketchup

**Directions:**
1. Combine ingredients in a saucepan. Heat over medium heat until the cranberry sauce melts and the sauce is warm.
2. Toss in drained meatballs and stir lightly to coat. Serve hot.

**Servings:** Entire recipe = 32 oz. lean protein + 2 C. veggies; ¼ recipe = 8 oz. lean protein + ½ C. veggies.

# Pork Recipes

## CINNAMON APPLE PORK TENDERLOIN
*Crockpot Recipe*

**Ingredients:**
1 lb. lean pork tenderloin
1 ¾ C. cubed chayote squash
1 T. dried minced onion
1 C. chicken broth (fat free, low sodium)
3 T. Walden Farms apple spread or (1 T. apple cider vinegar)
1 tsp. minced garlic
½ tsp. IP salt
1 tsp. yellow curry spice
1 tsp. onion powder
1 tsp. dry mustard
Cinnamon
2 tsp. olive oil

**Directions:**
1. Sprinkle cinnamon over entire pork tenderloin.
2. Heat a skillet on medium/medium high, add olive oil and heat.
3. Place tenderloin in skillet, sear until lightly browned on all sides, remove tenderloin from skillet and set aside.
4. Add cubed chayote to same skillet; stir fry approximately 5 minutes. Set aside.
5. In a small bowl, mix together the chicken broth, apple spread, garlic, salt, yellow curry, onion powder and dry mustard; set aside.
6. Place tenderloin in crockpot; add

dried minced onion and chayote. Pour the chicken broth mixture over the tenderloin.

7. Cook 5 hours on low. Season with salt and pepper, to taste.

**Servings:** Entire recipe = 16 oz. lean protein + 2 C. veggies; ½ recipe = 8 oz. lean protein + 1 C. veggies

## KALUA PORK & CABBAGE
*Crockpot recipe*

**Ingredients:**
3 lb. pork tenderloin roast
1 tsp. kosher salt
1 tsp. black pepper
1 tsp. garlic powder
2 tsp. dried minced onion
1 tsp. dried ginger powder
3 T. soy sauce
1/3 C. chicken broth, fat free
1 tsp. liquid smoke flavoring
3 C. shredded green cabbage
3 C. shredded red cabbage

**Directions:**
1. Mix together all dry spices and rub over entire pork roast. Place roast in crockpot.
2. In a small bowl, stir together soy sauce, chicken broth and liquid smoke flavoring. Pour over pork roast.
3. Cover and cook 7 hours on low.
4. Remove roast; add cabbage and stir to coat with juices. Place roast back in crockpot and cover; continue cooking one more hour or until done.
5. Serve by slicing pork into steaks and top with cabbage. Drizzle with juice from crockpot.

**Servings:** Entire recipe = 3 lb. lean protein + 6 C. veggies; 1/6 recipe = 8 oz. lean protein + 1 C. veggies

## MELT-IN-YOUR-MOUTH PORK TENDERLOIN
*Crockpot recipe*

**Ingredients:**
1 lb. lean pork tenderloin
¼ C. soy sauce
1 ½ T. Dijon mustard
4 tsp. olive oil
3 T. Walden Farms pancake syrup
1 T. + 1 ½ tsp. dried minced onions
1 tsp. onion powder
1 ½ tsp. garlic powder

**Directions:**
1. In a medium mixing bowl, combine all ingredients except pork; stir to mix.
2. Place pork tenderloin in crockpot; pour marinade over pork.
3. Cook on low 5 hours, turning tenderloin once during cooking.
4. Slice and serve, pouring desired amount of marinade over the pork.

**Servings:** Entire recipe = 16 oz. lean protein + 1/3 C. veggies; ½ recipe = 8 oz. lean protein + 2 ½ T. veggies

## PORK CARNITAS
*Crockpot recipe*

**Ingredients:**
3 lb. pork loin boneless center cut roast
1 tsp. garlic powder
1 tsp. ground cumin
1 tsp. salt
½ tsp. dried oregano leaves
½ tsp. ground coriander
¼ tsp. cinnamon
1 ½ C. chicken broth (fat free, low sodium)

**Directions:**
1. Mix together all the seasonings in a small bowl.
2. Rub the seasoning mixture over the pork roast, using your hands, making sure entire roast is coated.
3. Place the pork roast in a crockpot; pour the chicken broth around the sides of the roast being careful not to rinse off the spice mixture.
4. Cover and cook on low 10 hours; turn the roast after it has cooked 5 hours.
5. Shred the pork with 2 forks and serve. Use broth to moisten meat if needed, otherwise, discard remaining broth.

**Servings:** Entire recipe - 3 lbs. lean protein; 1/6 recipe = 8 oz. lean protein

**TIP:** Serve pork carnitas with the Tortilla Wraps (pg. 34) and Mockamole (pg. 50), or use meat to make sliders with any of the bread recipes in this cookbook.

## PORK FRIED RICE

**Ingredients:**
6 oz. pork tenderloin (cooked), cubed
1 ¾ C. (6.1 oz.) cauliflower florets, riced
¼ C. chopped green onion
1 - 2 tsp. olive oil
Garlic powder, to taste
2 - 3 T. chicken broth (fat free, low sodium)
1 egg, lightly beaten
Soy sauce, to taste
Black pepper

**Directions:**

1. Heat oil in a frying pan over medium/medium high heat. When the oil is hot, add the riced cauliflower. Stir fry approximately 7 minutes, or until lightly browned. Add the chicken broth 1 T. at a time to prevent the pan from getting dry.
2. Add the chopped green onion and garlic powder; stir fry 3 minutes or until the cauliflower rice is tender and lightly browned.
3. Pour beaten egg into the pan with the rice and stir fry until cooked, approximately 1 - 2 minutes.
4. Add pork and heat through.
5. Serve with black pepper and soy sauce.

**Servings:** 8 oz. lean protein (6 oz. pork + 2 oz. egg) + 2 C. veggies.

## SAUSAGE ZUCCHINI LASAGNA

**Ingredients:**

**8 oz. lean ground pork, beef, turkey or chicken**
**½ recipe Sausage Seasoning, pg. 51**
**2 C. (10.6 oz) zucchini, thinly sliced lengthwise in long strips**
**Salt for zucchini**
**10 oz. can diced tomatoes and chiles (undrained)**
**¼ tsp. garlic powder**
**¼ tsp. Italian seasoning**
**4 eggs**
**1/3 C. liquid egg whites (or 2 egg whites)**
**Pinch cayenne pepper, optional**
**Cooking spray**

**Directions:**

1. Preheat oven to 350 degrees.
2. Using a mandoline, slice zucchini lengthwise into thin long strips. Place strips in a large colander in the sink. Sprinkle strips lightly with salt and toss so salt covers most of the zucchini. Let rest while preparing remaining recipe. (This will take the moisture out of the zucchini so the lasagna won't be watery.)
3. In a medium frying pan, brown lean ground meat seasoned with Sausage Seasoning. Drain any fat; set aside.
4. Place the diced tomatoes and chiles, garlic powder, Italian seasoning and cayenne pepper in a blender; blend well. Set aside.
5. In a medium bowl, lightly beat together the 4 eggs + liquid egg whites. Set aside.
6. Spray an 8" x 8" square baking pan with cooking spray.
7. Remove zucchini strips from colander, blot with paper towels. Layer ½ the zucchini strips, covering the bottom of the baking pan.
8. Layer ½ the seasoned meat, spreading evenly.
9. Pour ½ the tomato mixture evenly over the meat.
10. Pour ½ the egg mixture evenly over the tomato mixture.
11. Repeat these layers, in order, with remaining ingredients.
12. Bake 40 minutes.

**Servings:** Entire recipe = 16 oz. lean protein + 4 C. veggies; ½ recipe = 8 oz. lean protein + 2 C. veggies

## YUM YUM GLAZED PORK CHOPS

*Rosemary, apricot and Dijon flavors*

**2 - 8 oz. boneless pork loin chops (1" thick)**
**1 tsp. dried crushed rosemary**
**1 tsp. garlic powder**
**Salt and pepper, to taste**
**1 T. olive oil**
**1 T. Dijon mustard**
**1 T. Walden Farms apricot or apple spread**
**1 tsp. soy sauce**
**Cooking spray**

**Directions:**

1. Preheat oven to 350 degrees.
2. Put Dijon mustard, apricot (or apple) spread and soy sauce in a small bowl; microwave on high 25 seconds. Stir with a fork till mixed; set aside.
3. Season chops by sprinkling rosemary, garlic powder, salt and pepper on both sides.
4. Heat olive oil on a grill pan (or fry pan) over medium/medium high heat until hot. Add chops to hot pan and grill 3 minutes each side.
5. Place chops in a sprayed 8"x 8" baking dish. Pour Dijon mixture over chops; bake 25 minutes or until internal temperature reaches 145 degrees. Let rest 3 minutes before serving.

**Servings:** Entire recipe = 16 oz. lean protein; ½ recipe = 8 oz. lean protein

# Beverages & Smoothies

**TIP:** A 900 watt minimum bullet style blender is recommended for many of the smoothie recipes using ice. It will make the texture turn smooth and creamy without the icy bits left behind.

Add spinach to your smoothie; the taste is easily overridden with other flavors and it's a great way to get some veggies in for the day. Add ice a little at a time to help prevent a foamy texture.

Perk up smoothie flavors by adding spices such as cinnamon, nutmeg, sugar free extracts and Walden Farms syrups and spreads, to taste. The flavor combinations are endless; the variety will keep your interest.

**Cinna-Vanilla Iced Coffee**
**Page 15**

**Coconut Almond Hot Chocolate**
**Page 15**

**Peanut Butter Cup Smoothie**
**Page 17**

## APPLE PIE SMOOTHIE

Ingredients:
8 - 10 oz. cold water
1 IP vanilla pudding mix (dry)
2 heaping T. Walden Farms apple butter spread
¼ tsp. apple pie spice
(or cinnamon)
¼ tsp. butter extract
(or vanilla extract)
2 C. ice

Directions:
1. Place all ingredients (except ice) in a 900+ watt blender; blend well.
2. Add 1 C. ice and blend; add remaining ice and blend to desired consistency.

Servings:  1 unrestricted

TIP:  The Walden Farms apple butter does not dissolve easily.  Microwave for 5 seconds and stir before adding to the smoothie, making it easier to blend.

## BANANA SPLIT ICE CREAM SMOOTHIE

*Vanilla, strawberry, chocolate, banana and pineapple*

Ingredients:
½ IP *vanilla premade drink (see tip below to get exactly ½ the drink measurement)
½ IP *strawberry-banana premade drink
2 T. Walden Farms chocolate syrup
¼ tsp. *pineapple extract (optional)
1 C. ice

Directions:
1. Place all ingredients in a blender; blend on high until smooth and creamy.

Servings:  1 unrestricted

TIP:  *To measure exactly ½ of each IP drink, pour the entire contents of both drinks into a glass 4 C. measuring cup; whisk to blend.  You will have 2 ½ C. total. Pour 1 ¼ C. of mix into the blender; store remaining vanilla/strawberry-banana drink blend in refrigerator for another serving/meal.  You may pour it back into the vanilla drink bottle and label the bottle's contents.  The pineapple extract may be purchased at www.olivenation.com.

## BRANDIED COFFEE VELVET SMOOTHIE

Ingredients:
1 IP cappuccino drink mix (dry)
2 T. Walden Farms chocolate syrup
¼ tsp.*brandy extract, sugar free
4 oz. cold water
1 C. ice

Directions:
1. Place all ingredients, except ice, in a 900+ watt blender; blend well.
2. Add ice; blend to desired consistency.

Servings:  1 unrestricted

TIP:  *You may purchase brandy extract at www.olivenation.com.  For a stronger brandy taste, ½ tsp. brandy extract may be used.  Taste the smoothie first using ¼ tsp. before adding more.

## CARAMEL CHEESECAKE SMOOTHIE

Ingredients:
1 IP vanilla drink mix (dry)
½ C. cold water
2 T. Walden Farms caramel syrup
1 tsp. *cream cheese emulsion,

optional
Cinnamon, to taste
1 C. ice

Directions:
1.  Blend all ingredients, except ice, in a 900+ watt blender.
2.  Add ice; blend well.

Servings:  1 unrestricted

TIP:  *You may purchase the cream cheese emulsion at www.olivenation.com.

## CARAMEL VANILLA SMOOTHIE

Ingredients:
1 IP vanilla pudding mix (dry)
2 T. Walden Farms caramel syrup
1 tsp. vanilla extract
8 - 10 oz. water
1 C. ice

Directions:
1.  Blend ingredients, except ice, in a 900+ watt blender.
2.  Add ice and blend well.

Servings:  1 unrestricted

## CHOCOLATE ALMOND SMOOTHIE

Ingredients:
1 IP dark chocolate pudding mix (dry)
10 oz. cold water
2 T. almond coffee syrup, sugar free
(or ¼ tsp. almond extract)
2 C. ice, divided

Directions:
1.  Blend ingredients, except ice, in a 900+ watt blender.
2.  Add 1 C. ice and blend well; add additional 1 C. ice and blend to desired consistency.

Servings:  1 unrestricted

## CHOCOLATE COCONUT ALMOND ICED LATTE

**Ingredients:**
1 IP vanilla pre-made drink
2 oz. espresso, cold (or strong coffee)
1 T. Walden Farms chocolate syrup
1/8 tsp. coconut extract
1/8 tsp. almond extract
Ice cubes

**Directions:**
1. Mix together; pour over ice.

**Servings:** 1 unrestricted

**TIP:** Pour cold coffee into an ice cube tray and freeze; using the coffee cubes ensures a rich latte to the end.

## CHOCOLATE COVERED CHERRY SMOOTHIE

**Ingredients:**
1 IP dark chocolate pudding mix (dry)
¼ tsp. *cherry extract, sugar free
8 oz. cold water
2 C. ice, divided

**Directions:**
1. Blend ingredients, except ice, in a 900+ watt blender.
2. Add 1 C. ice and blend well; add additional 1 C. ice and blend to desired consistency.

**Servings:** 1 unrestricted

**TIP:** *You may purchase cherry extract at www.olivenation.com.

## CHOCOLATE FUDGE RHUBARB SMOOTHIE

**Ingredients:**
1 IP chocolate drink mix (dry)
1 C. Strawberry Rhubarb Compote, pg. 45
6 oz. cold water
1 tsp. *Fudge Brownie flavor fountain, optional
2 C. ice cubes

**Directions:**
1. Place the first four ingredients in a high speed blender; blend well.
2. Add the ice and blend until smooth and creamy.

**Servings:** 1 unrestricted + 2 C. veggies (1 C. compote = 2 C. veggies)

**TIP:** *You may purchase the Fudge Brownie flavor fountain at www.olivenation.com; the smoothie will have a richer chocolate taste. However, you may sub 1 T. Walden Farms chocolate syrup as an alternative, or leave out entirely if you choose.

## CINNA-VANILLA ICED COFFEE

**Ingredients:**
2 oz. cold espresso (or cold strong coffee)
1 IP vanilla pre-made drink
½ tsp. cinnamon
¼ tsp. sugar-free sweetener, granular

**Directions:**
1. Mix together; pour over ice.

**Servings:** 1 unrestricted

**TIP:** Pour additional cold coffee into an ice cube tray and freeze; using the coffee cubes ensures a rich latte to the end.

## COCONUT ALMOND HOT CHOCOLATE

**Ingredients:**
1 IP chocolate drink mix (dry)
8 oz. water
1/8 tsp. coconut extract
1/8 tsp. almond extract
1 heaping tsp. Walden Farms marshmallow dip

**Directions:**
1. Place chocolate drink mix, water, coconut extract and almond extract in a blender; blend.
2. Pour into a mug; heat in microwave until hot.
3. Top with Walden Farms marshmallow dip.

**Servings:** 1 unrestricted

## COFFEE AND DOUGHNUTS ICE CREAM SMOOTHIE

**Ingredients:**
1 IP vanilla pudding mix (dry)
½ tsp. butter extract
¼ tsp. coffee extract
¼ tsp. cinnamon
10 oz. cold water
2 C. ice

**Directions:**
1. Blend ingredients, except ice, in a 900+ watt blender. The longer it is blended, the thicker it will be for an ice cream-like texture.
2. Add ice and blend well to desired consistency.

**Servings:** 1 unrestricted

**TIP:** The butter and coffee extracts can be found at local large discount retailers or grocery stores.

## COFFEE-HOUSE ICED LATTE

**Ingredients:**
1 IP vanilla pre-made drink (or another flavor)
2 shots espresso
Sugar free coffee syrup (any flavor)
Cinnamon (optional)

**Directions:**
1. When ordering coffee at a coffee house, ask for a double shot of espresso over ice in a Venti cup with 1 - 2 pumps sugar free coffee syrup.
2. Add the IP pre-made drink; sprinkle with cinnamon. Stir to mix.

**Servings:** 1 unrestricted

**TIP:** For a hot café latte, ask the barista if he/she can steam the IP pre-made drink in place of milk.

## CRAN-ORANGE SMOOTHIE

**Ingredients:**
1 IP vanilla pudding mix (dry)
8 - 10 oz. cold water
1 T. Walden Farms cranberry spread
1 T. Walden Farms orange marmalade spread
2 C. ice

**Directions:**
1. Blend ingredients, except ice, in a 900+ watt blender. The longer it is blended, the thicker it will be for an ice cream-like texture.
2. Add ice and blend well to desired consistency.

**Servings:** 1 unrestricted

**TIP:** This smoothie has helped me get through the holidays without a cheat; it may have a holiday flavor but tastes great anytime.

## DARK CHOCOLATE COCONUT SMOOTHIE

**Ingredients:**
1 IP dark chocolate pudding mix (dry)
8 - 10 oz. water
½ tsp. coconut extract, sugar free (or 2 T. coconut coffee syrup, sugar free)
2 C. ice

**Directions:**
1. Blend ingredients, except ice, in a 900+ watt blender. The longer it is blended, the thicker it will be for an ice cream-like texture.
2. Add ice and blend well to desired consistency.

**Servings:** 1 unrestricted

## EGGNOG

**Ingredients:**
1 IP pre-made vanilla drink
1 ½ tsp. IP vanilla pudding mix, dry
1/8 tsp. rum extract
¼ tsp. nutmeg

**Directions:**
1. Place all ingredients in a blender; blend. Serve over ice.

**Servings:** 1 unrestricted

**TIP:** The use of the 1 ½ tsp. vanilla pudding mix is not enough to count as a full serving; count as an 'extra' for the day such as sugar free sweetener.

## EGGNOG SMOOTHIE

**Ingredients:**
1 IP vanilla pudding mix (dry)
8 - 10 oz. cold water
¼ tsp. nutmeg
¼ tsp. rum extract, sugar free
¼ tsp. vanilla extract

1 tsp. sugar free sweetener, granulated
2 C. ice

**Directions:**
1. Blend ingredients, except ice, in a 900+ watt blender. The longer it is blended, the thicker it will be for an ice cream-like texture.
2. Add ice and blend well to desired consistency.

**Servings:** 1 unrestricted

## ELVIS SMOOTHIE

**Ingredients:**
1 IP vanilla pudding mix (dry)
2 heaping T. Walden Farms peanut butter
8 - 10 oz. water
½ tsp. banana extract
1 ½ C. ice

**Directions:**
1. Blend ingredients, except ice, in a 900+ watt blender. The longer it is blended, the thicker it will be for an ice cream-like texture.
2. Add ice and blend well to desired consistency.

**Servings:** 1 unrestricted

## FROZEN CHOCOLATE CARAMEL MACCHIATO

**Ingredients:**
1 IP cappuccino drink mix (dry)
1 T. Walden Farms chocolate syrup
1 - 2 T. Walden Farms caramel syrup
4 oz. cold coffee
1 C. ice

**Directions:**
1. Place all ingredients, except ice, in a 900+ watt blender; blend well.
2. Add ice; blend to desired consistency.

**Servings:** 1 unrestricted

# FROZEN SPINACH ICE CUBES
*For Smoothies*

**Ingredients:**
4 C. fresh spinach
Water to blend

**Directions:**
1.  Wash spinach.
2.  Add 1 C. water to your 900+ watt blender; a standard blender will not work as well for this recipe.
3.  Add 2 C. spinach to your blender and pulse until the spinach is pulverized.  Continue to add remaining spinach, blending briefly after each addition.
4.  Blend spinach mixture for a minute or until smooth, adding more water if necessary.
5.  Pour mixture into molds.  I use muffin tins, mini muffin tins or ice cube trays.  If using the larger muffin tins, the cubes may not blend as easily once frozen.  Silicone muffin tins make it easy to remove the frozen cubes.
6.  Put muffin tin/ice cube trays in the freezer; freeze.
7.  Remove frozen spinach cubes from tins or trays, place the frozen cubes in a resealable bag and return to freezer for storage.

**Servings:**  Entire recipe = 4 C. veggies; ½ recipe = 2 C. veggies

**TIPS:**  Using the spinach ice cubes keeps fresh spinach from spoiling and your smoothie cold.  The cubes may be added to hot soup for additional veggies.

# HAZELNUT MOCHACCINO SMOOTHIE

**Ingredients:**
1 IP cappuccino drink mix (dry)
4 oz. strong cold coffee
1 T. Walden Farms chocolate syrup
2 T. hazelnut coffee syrup, sugar free
1 C. ice

**Directions:**
1.  Blend ingredients, except ice, in a 900+ watt blender.
2.  Add ice and blend well to desired consistency.

**Servings:**  1 unrestricted

# LEMON CHIFFON SMOOTHIE

**Ingredients:**
1 IP vanilla pudding mix (dry)
8 - 10 oz. water
¼ tsp. lemon extract, sugar free
2 heaping T. Walden Farms marshmallow dip
2 C. ice

**Directions:**
1.  Blend ingredients, except ice, in a 900+ watt blender.  The longer it is blended, the thicker it will be for an ice cream-like texture.
2.  Add ice and blend well to desired consistency.

**Servings:**  1 unrestricted

# MINT CHOCOLATE CHIP SMOOTHIE

**Ingredients:**
1 IP vanilla drink mix (dry)
¼ tsp. mint extract
3 drops green food coloring
½ C. cold water
1 C. ice
1 IP packet chocolate soy puffs, lightly crushed

**Directions:**
1.  Place water, mint extract and food coloring in blender; pulse to blend.  Add vanilla drink mix; blend.
2.  Add ice; blend until completely smooth.  Check consistency and add more water or ice as needed.
3.  Stir chocolate soy puffs into

smoothie; pour into a tall glass and serve.

**Servings:**  2 unrestricted

**TIP:**  Freeze 1/2 the smoothie for another serving.  Blend in blender when ready to serve.

# ORANGE CREAMSICLE SMOOTHIE

**Ingredients:**
1 IP vanilla drink mix (dry)
2 T. Walden Farms orange marmalade
1 tsp. cream cheese emulsion (optional)
4 oz. cold water
1 C. ice

**Directions:**
1.  Blend ingredients, except ice, in a 900+ watt blender.
2.  Add ice and blend well to desired consistency.

**Servings:**  1 unrestricted

**TIP:**  You may purchase the cream cheese emulsion from www.olivenation.com.

# PEANUT BUTTER CUP SMOOTHIE

**Ingredients:**
1 IP chocolate drink mix (dry)
2 T. Walden Farms peanut butter
½ tsp. vanilla extract
4 oz. water
1 C. ice

**Directions:**
1.  Blend ingredients, except ice, in a 900+ watt blender.
2.  Add ice and blend well to desired consistency.

**Servings:**  1 unrestricted

## PEPPERMINT MOCHA FRAPPUCCINO

Ingredients:
1 IP chocolate drink mix (dry)
2 T. Walden Farms chocolate syrup
5 oz. strong coffee, cold
¼ tsp. peppermint extract
1 C. ice

Directions:
1. Blend ingredients, except ice, in a 900+ watt blender.
2. Add ice and blend well to desired consistency.

Servings: 1 unrestricted

TIP: Mint extract may be substituted for the peppermint extract.

## ROOTBEER FLOAT SMOOTHIE

Ingredients:
1 IP vanilla drink mix (dry)
4 oz. cold water
¼ tsp. vanilla extract
¼ tsp. rootbeer extract, sugar free
1 C. ice

Directions:
1. Blend ingredients, except ice, in a 900+ watt blender.
2. Add ice and blend well.

Servings: 1 unrestricted

TIP: Rootbeer extract is available at large discount retailers and many grocery stores.

Directions:
1. Put all ingredients, except ice, in a 900+ watt blender. Blend well.
2. Add ice and blend thoroughly.

Servings: 1 unrestricted

TIP: You may purchase the emulsions from www.olivenation.com and find them essential for a great tiramisu flavor. However, a good substitute for the cream cheese and brandy emulsions would be 1 tsp. vanilla extract + ¼ tsp. rum extract.

## PUMPKIN LATTE FRAPPE

Ingredients:
1 IP vanilla pudding mix (dry)
8 - 10 oz. cold strong coffee
½ tsp. pumpkin pie spice
1 tsp. vanilla extract
½ tsp. sugar free sweetener, granular
1 T. Walden Farms caramel syrup, optional
2 C. ice

Directions:
1. Blend ingredients, except ice, in a 900+ watt blender. The longer it is blended, the thicker it will be for an ice cream-like texture.
2. Add ice and blend well to desired consistency.

Servings: 1 unrestricted

TIP: Flavored coffee works nicely in this recipe; I use a Caramel Drizzle flavor.

## STRAWBERRY SHORTCAKE SMOOTHIE

Ingredients:
1 IP vanilla drink mix (dry)
4 oz. cold water
1 T. Walden Farms strawberry syrup
½ tsp. vanilla or strawberry extract
¼ tsp. butter extract
1 C. ice

Directions:
1. Blend all ingredients, except ice, in a 900+ watt blender.
2. Add ice; blend well.

Servings: 1 unrestricted

## TIRAMISU SMOOTHIE

Ingredients:
1 IP cappuccino drink mix (dry)
4 oz. cold water
1 T. Walden Farms chocolate syrup
1 tsp. cream cheese emulsion (see tip below)
¼ tsp. brandy emulsion (see tip below)
1 C. ice

## TROPICAL SHERBET SMOOTHIE

*Janeva's favorite smoothie Vanilla, mango, strawberry and coconut*

Ingredients:
½ IP *vanilla premade drink (see tip below to get exactly ½ the drink measurement)
½ IP *mango premade drink
1 T. Walden Farms strawberry syrup
¼ tsp. coconut extract
1 C. ice

Directions:
1. Place all ingredients in a blender; blend on high until smooth and creamy.

Servings: 1 unrestricted

TIP: *To measure exactly ½ of each IP drink, pour the entire contents of both drinks into a glass 4 C. measuring cup; whisk to blend. You will have 2 C. total. Pour 1 C. of mix into the blender; store remaining vanilla-mango drink blend in refrigerator for another serving/meal. You may pour it back into the vanilla drink bottle and label the bottle's contents.

# Breads, Muffins & Wraps

**BAKING TIPS:**

1.   It is good habit to read the entire recipe before beginning to ensure a satisfactory finish.
2.   Spray coat muffin/baking pans prior to adding the batter; the baked goods will come out of the pans easily making clean-up a cinch.
3.   Do not use baking cup liners for the muffins/cupcakes as they will stick to the baked goods. Parchment liners are acceptable.
4.   Always use precise measurements when baking, it is a science of ingredients that needs to be exact.
5.   Follow the directions as stated in the recipe.  It is important the dry ingredients are mixed together before adding the liquid ingredients.
6.   Use fresh baking powder and bake immediately after mixing the batter, or the baking powder will deactivate.
7.   In most cases, 1/3 C. liquid egg whites = 2 egg whites. If using real egg whites, make sure to whisk lightly before adding to the batter.

**Glazed Lemon Zucchini Scones**
**Page 28**

**Cinnamon & Sugar Toast**
**Page 25**

**Breakfast Buzz Muffins**
**Page 21**

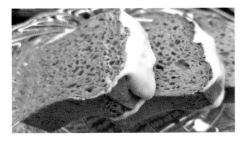

**Gingerbread**
**Page 28**

**Strawberry Rhubarb Oatmeal**
**Muffins - Page 33**

**Garlic Zucchini Bagels**
**Page 27**

*www.JanevasIdealRecipes.com*

# APPLE BUTTER OATMEAL MUFFINS

**Ingredients:**
1 IP apple oatmeal mix (dry)
1 IP crispy cereal mix (dry), crushed
2 tsp. baking powder
1/3 C. liquid egg whites
1 tsp. olive oil
¼ tsp. sugar free sweetener, granular
1 T. Walden Farms apple butter
Cooking spray

**Directions:**
1. Preheat oven to 350 degrees.
2. In a medium mixing bowl, mix together the apple oatmeal, crispy cereal, baking powder and sweetener.
3. Heat apple butter in a small dish in the microwave for 8 - 10 seconds; stir to mix. Add the apple butter, liquid egg whites and olive oil to the dry mixture and stir until incorporated.
4. Spray a regular size muffin tin with cooking spray; scoop batter into 4 muffin tins.
5. Bake 15 minutes.

**Servings:** 4 muffins = 2 unrestricted; 2 muffins = 1 unrestricted

**TIP:** Serve with warmed Walden Farms apple butter or drizzle with Walden Farms caramel syrup.

# APPLE FRITTER MUFFINS

**Ingredients:**
1 package IP apple cinnamon soy puffs, crushed
1 IP plain pancake mix (dry)
1 tsp. baking powder
1/3 C. liquid egg whites
2 T. Walden Farms or IP pancake syrup
¼ C. Zucchini Fried Apples, finely chopped (pg. 46), or *shredded zucchini

**Directions:**
1. Preheat oven to 350 degrees.
2. In a medium bowl, mix the dry ingredients.
3. Add the remaining ingredients; stir to mix.
4. Spray a jumbo muffin tin (Texas size) with cooking spray; spoon batter into muffin tin making 2 jumbo muffins. (If you do not have a Texas jumbo muffin tin, use a regular size muffin tin making 6 muffins; Bake 8-10 minutes. Eat 3 muffins for same serving equivalent to 1 jumbo muffin.)
5. Bake jumbo muffins 10-12 minutes.

**Servings:** 2 muffins = 1 unrestricted + 1 restricted + ¼ C. veggies; 1 muffin = ½ unrestricted + ½ restricted + 1/8 C. veggies

**TIP:** If eating one muffin as a meal in one day, I would count this as a restricted for that day (even though it's ½ restricted + ½ unrestricted).
*If using shredded zucchini, heat in microwave on high for 1 minute; blot with paper towels before adding to batter.

# APPLE JAX MUFFINS

**Ingredients:**
1 IP apple or maple oatmeal mix (dry)
1 tsp. baking powder
¼ tsp. cinnamon
2 T. liquid egg whites
2 T. Walden Farms pancake syrup
Cooking spray

**Directions:**
1. Preheat oven to 350 degrees.
2. In a medium bowl, mix dry ingredients. Add liquid ingredients; stir to mix.
3. Spray a regular size muffin tin with cooking spray; spoon batter into muffin tin making 3 muffins.
4. Bake 10 minutes.

**Servings:** 1 unrestricted

# BACON CHEDDAR BREAD

**Ingredients:**
1 IP bacon & cheddar cheese omelet mix (dry)
1 IP potato puree (dry)
1 tsp. baking powder
1 egg, large
1 tsp. olive oil
¼ C. water
Cooking spray

**Directions:**
1. Preheat oven to 350 degrees.
2. In a medium bowl, mix dry ingredients.
3. Add liquid ingredients; stir to mix.
4. Pour batter into a sprayed standard size 9"x 5"x 2 ½" loaf pan.
5. Bake 6-8 minutes, or until an inserted toothpick comes clean; cool completely (this is necessary for texture).
6. Slice entire loaf in half; then slice horizontally into 2 slices of bread. Toast lightly in toaster for best results.

**Servings:** Entire loaf = 2 unrestricted + 2 oz. lean protein; ½ loaf = 1 unrestricted + 1 oz. lean protein.

**TIP:** Picture shown includes 2 fried eggs (add 4 oz. protein); makes a great bacon, egg and cheese flavored sandwich.

# BANANA APPLE OATMEAL MUFFINS

**Ingredients:**
1 IP vanilla pudding mix (dry)
1 IP apple oatmeal mix (dry)
2 tsp. baking powder
½ tsp. banana extract
1/3 C. liquid egg whites
1 tsp. olive oil
2 T. Walden Farms apple butter spread (or pancake syrup or caramel syrup)
¼ C. water
Cooking spray

**Directions:**
1. Preheat oven to 350 degrees.
2. In a medium bowl, mix dry ingredients together. Add liquid ingredients; stir to mix. Heat the Walden Farms apple butter spread in the microwave for 15 seconds on high to soften before adding to batter; stir. (If using the syrup, there is no need to warm.)
3. Spray a regular size muffin tin with cooking spray. Scoop batter into tin making 4 muffins.
4. Bake 16 - 20 minutes or until an inserted toothpick comes out clean. I check at 16 minutes and every minute after that.

**Servings:** 4 muffins = 2 unrestricted; 2 muffins = 1 unrestricted

# BANANA CHOCOLATE CHIP MUFFINS

**Ingredients:**
1 IP vanilla pudding mix (dry)
1 IP chocolate chip pancake mix (dry)
1 tsp. baking powder
1 tsp. sugar free sweetener, granular
1/3 C. liquid egg whites
2 tsp. olive oil
¼ tsp. banana extract
4 T. water
Cooking spray

**Directions:**
1. Preheat oven to 350 degrees.
2. In a medium bowl, mix together the dry ingredients.
3. Add liquid ingredients; stir to mix.
4. Spray a regular size muffin tin with cooking spray; spoon batter into muffin tin making 6 muffins.
5. Bake 10 - 12 minutes.

**Servings:** 6 muffins = 2 unrestricted; 3 muffins = 1 unrestricted

# BANANAS FOSTER MUFFIN BREAD

**Ingredients:**
1 IP vanilla pudding mix (dry)
1 IP maple oatmeal mix (dry)
2 tsp. baking powder
¼ tsp. cinnamon
1/3 c. liquid egg whites
1 T. milk
2 tsp. olive oil
1/8 tsp. rum extract
¼ tsp. banana extract
2 T. Walden Farms caramel syrup
1/4 C. water
Cooking spray

**Directions:**
1. Preheat oven to 350 degrees.
2. In a medium bowl, mix dry ingredients together. Add liquid ingredients; stir to mix.
3. Put batter into a sprayed 5 3/8" x 3" x 2 1/8" mini loaf pan.
4. Bake 20 - 23 minutes or until an inserted toothpick comes out clean.

**Servings:** Entire recipe = 2 unrestricted; ½ recipe = 1 unrestricted

**TIP:** Makes excellent French toast. See French Toast recipe, pg. 63.

# BREAKFAST BUZZ MUFFINS
*Coffee, espresso and chocolate*

**Ingredients:**
1 IP chocolatey caramel mug cake (dry)
1 IP maple oatmeal (dry)
1 T. instant coffee espresso powder
1 tsp. cinnamon or pumpkin pie spice
1 tsp. baking powder
2 large eggs, slightly beaten
¼ C. cold coffee
1 C. shredded zucchini
Cooking spray

**Directions:**
1. Preheat oven to 350 degrees.
2. Place zucchini in a small bowl; microwave on high 30 seconds. Blot with paper towel to absorb excess moisture; set aside.
3. In a medium bowl, mix together dry ingredients.
4. In a separate medium bowl, mix together liquid ingredients including zucchini.
5. Pour liquid mixture into dry mixture; stir to combine.
6. Spray a standard sized muffin tin and fill, making 6 muffins.
7. Bake 14 – 16 minutes or until an inserted toothpick comes out clean.
8. Cool completely or muffins will be spongy.

**Servings:** 6 muffins = 2 unrestricted + 1 C. veggies + 4 oz. lean protein; 3 muffins = 1 unrestricted + ½ C. veggies + 2 oz. lean protein

# BROCCOLI CHEESE LOAF BREAD

**Ingredients:**
1 IP broccoli cheese soup mix (dry)

1 IP crispy cereal mix (dry), crushed
2 tsp. baking powder
¼ tsp. Italian seasoning
¼ tsp. garlic powder
1/8 tsp. onion powder
Pinch of IP salt
1/3 C. liquid egg whites
¼ C. milk
2 tsp. olive oil
Cooking spray

Directions:
1. Preheat oven to 350 degrees.
2. In a medium bowl, mix together dry ingredients.
3. Add the liquid ingredients; stir to mix.
4. Pour batter into a sprayed 5 3/8" x 3" x 2 1/8" mini loaf pan.
5. Bake for 18 - 20 minutes or until an inserted toothpick comes out clean.

Servings: Entire loaf = 2 unrestricted; ½ loaf = 1 unrestricted

TIP: Makes a great side with soup and/or salad. Toast slices lightly in toaster for slider buns.

## BROCCOLI CHEESE PITA BREAD WRAP

Ingredients:
1 IP broccoli cheese soup mix (dry)
1/3 c. liquid egg whites
1 tsp. olive oil
¼ tsp. baking powder
¼ tsp. garlic powder (or onion powder)
Cooking spray

Directions:
1. In a bowl, blend dry ingredients. Add liquid ingredients; mix well.
2. Spray an 8-inch frying pan with cooking spray and heat on medium heat. Spread mixture in pan. Batter will be thick; spread it into a 6"+ circle with the back of a sprayed

spoon.
3. Cook until edges look dry and bottom of pita is browned, approximately 2 minutes; flip and continue cooking for 30 seconds or until browned.

Servings: 1 unrestricted

TIP: Stuff with veggies and/or meat and fold; for a variation, make two separate round buns.

## BROCCOLI CHEESE WAFFLE BURGER BUNS

Ingredients:
1 IP broccoli cheese soup mix (dry)
1 IP crispy cereal mix (dry), crushed
1/8 tsp. baking powder
2 T. liquid egg whites
2 T. milk
1 T. water
2 tsp. olive oil
Garlic powder, to taste
Cooking spray

Directions:
1. In a medium bowl, mix together the dry ingredients.
2. Add liquid ingredients; stir to mix.
3. Preheat waffle iron, coat with cooking spray; fill with batter and bake according to waffle iron manufacturer directions. Makes 4 waffles.

Servings: 4 waffle buns = 2 unrestricted; 2 waffle buns = 1 unrestricted

TIP: May be used for hamburger or other sandwich bun; any remaining waffle buns may be reheated lightly in the toaster. Other soup mixes may be substituted providing a different flavor.

## CANDIED ALMOND COFFEE CAKE

Ingredients:
1 IP crispy cereal mix (dry), crushed
1 IP vanilla pudding mix (dry)
2 tsp. baking powder
½ tsp. cinnamon
1 tsp. sugar free sweetener, granular
1/3 C. liquid egg whites
2 tsp. olive oil
2 T. Walden Farms caramel syrup
½ tsp. almond extract
Cooking spray

Directions:
1. Preheat oven to 350 degrees.
2. In a medium mixing bowl, blend dry ingredients. Add liquid ingredients; stir to mix.
3. Pour batter into sprayed 5 3/8" x 3" x 2 1/8" mini loaf pan. Pat down batter lightly and evenly with the back of a sprayed spoon.
4. Bake for 16 - 19 minutes or until an inserted toothpick comes out clean.

Servings: Entire loaf = 2 unrestricted; ½ loaf = 1 unrestricted

## CARAMEL APPLE OATMEAL BREAD

Ingredients:
1 IP apple oatmeal mix (dry)
1 IP vanilla pudding mix (dry)
2 tsp. baking powder
1/3 C. liquid egg whites
3 T. milk
2 tsp. olive oil
½ tsp. apple pie spice
½ tsp. vanilla extract
1 T. Walden Farms caramel syrup
2 T. water
Cooking spray

Directions:
1. Preheat oven to 350 degrees.
2. In a medium mixing bowl, blend dry ingredients. Add liquid ingredients; stir to mix.
3. Pour batter into sprayed 5 3/8" x

3" x 2 1/8" mini loaf pan. Using the back of a sprayed spoon, spread batter evenly.

4. Bake for 20 - 23 minutes or until inserted toothpick comes out clean.

**Servings:** Entire loaf = 2 unrestricted; ½ loaf = 1 unrestricted

## CARAMEL ZUCCHINI MUFFINS

**Ingredients:**
1 IP chocolate chip pancake or plain pancake mix (dry)
¼ tsp. baking powder
2 T. liquid egg whites
2 T. Walden Farms caramel syrup
¼ C. shredded zucchini
Cooking spray

**Directions:**
1. Preheat oven to 350 degrees.
2. In a small microwave-proof bowl, cook shredded zucchini in the microwave on high for one minute. After cooking, blot with paper towels by pressing down on the cooked zucchini to eliminate as much of the moisture as possible.
3. Place the pancake mix in a medium bowl; add baking powder, making sure it is distributed throughout the mix.
4. Add the liquid egg whites and caramel syrup; stir to mix. Fold in shredded zucchini.
5. Spray a regular size muffin tin with cooking spray; spoon batter into muffin tin making 3 muffins.
6. Bake 10 minutes.

**Servings:** 1 unrestricted + ¼ C. veggies

## CHALUPA TACO WRAP

**Ingredients:**
1 IP potato puree mix (dry)
1 tsp. Taco Seasoning, pg. 52
1/3 C. liquid egg whites
1 tsp. olive oil
Cooking spray

**Directions:**
1. In a small bowl, mix dry ingredients together. Add liquid ingredients; stir to mix.
2. Heat a small frying pan over medium heat; spray with cooking spray. Add batter and spread into a large pancake size wrap with the back of a sprayed spoon.
3. Cook until browned; flip and cook the other side.

**Servings:** 1 unrestricted

**TIP:** Fill with 2 oz. taco seasoned ground beef, turkey or chicken. Top with lettuce and Pico de Gallo Salsa pg. 50; makes a great lunch.

## CHICKEN BISCUITS

**Ingredients:**
1 IP chicken soup mix (dry)
1 IP crispy cereal mix (dry), crushed
2 tsp. baking powder
¼ tsp. garlic powder
¼ tsp. onion powder
Pinch of IP salt
1/3 C. liquid egg whites
¼ C. (2 oz.) milk
2 tsp. olive oil
Cooking spray

**Directions:**
1. Preheat oven to 350 degrees.
2. In a medium mixing bowl, mix together the dry ingredients with a whisk.

3. Add liquid ingredients and stir to incorporate, just until mixed; over stirring the batter will make the biscuits tough.
4. Scoop batter into sprayed, regular size muffin tin making 6 biscuits.
5. Bake 10 - 12 minutes or until inserted toothpick comes out clean.

**Servings:** 6 biscuits = 2 unrestricted; 3 biscuits = 1 unrestricted

**TIP:** I split these by eating ½ the recipe one day and the other ½ recipe the following day (not in the same day.) This entire recipe takes up the milk allowance for two days.

## CHICKEN FAUX-CACCIA BREAD WRAP

**Ingredients:**
1 IP chicken patty mix (dry)
¼ tsp. baking powder
Garlic powder, to taste
¼ C. liquid egg whites
Cooking spray

**Directions:**
1. In a small mixing bowl, blend chicken patty mix, baking powder and garlic powder. Add liquid egg whites; stir to mix. Let mixture rest 5 minutes so chicken mix absorbs moisture.
2. Spray an 8-inch frying pan with cooking spray and heat on medium. Spread mixture in pan.
3. Cook until edges look dry and bottom of pita is browned; flip and continue cooking for 30 seconds or until browned.

**Servings:** 1 unrestricted

**TIP:** Stuff with veggies and/or meat and roll up or cut in half to make two slices for a sandwich. This makes a great pita bread for the Gyros recipe, pg. 84.

## CHOCOLATE CHIP CARAMEL MINI MUFFINS

**Ingredients:**
1 IP vanilla pudding mix (dry)
1 IP chocolate chip pancake mix (dry)

1 tsp. baking powder
1 tsp. sugar free sweetener, granular
1/3 C. liquid egg whites
1 tsp. olive oil
2 T. water
2 T. Walden Farms caramel syrup
Cooking spray

**Directions:**
1. Preheat oven to 350 degrees.
2. In a medium bowl, mix together the dry ingredients.
3. Add liquid ingredients; stir to mix.
4. Spoon batter into a sprayed mini muffin tin making 12 mufins.
5. Bake for 10 minutes or until an inserted toothpick comes clean.

**Servings:** 12 mini muffins = 2 unrestricted; 6 mini muffins = 1 unrestricted

# CHOCOLATE MINT LAVA LOAF

**Ingredients:**
1 IP dark chocolate pudding mix (dry)
1 IP crispy cereal mix (dry), crushed
2 tsp. baking powder
1 tsp. sugar free sweetener, granular
1/3 C. liquid egg whites
1 T. milk
2 tsp. olive oil
1 T. Walden Farms chocolate syrup
2 T. IP vanilla pre-made drink
1 IP chocolate mint bar, cut in 8 pieces
Cooking spray

**Directions:**
1. Preheat oven to 350 degrees.
2. In a medium sized mixing bowl, mix together dry ingredients except chocolate mint bar. Add liquid ingredients; stir to mix.
3. Fold chocolate mint bar pieces

into batter.
4. Spray a 5 3/8" x 3" x 2 1/8" mini loaf pan with cooking spray and add batter. Lightly pat down with the back of a sprayed spoon to even out.
5. Bake for 15 - 20 minutes or until toothpick inserted comes out clean.

**Servings:** Entire loaf = 2 unrestricted + 1 restricted

**TIP:** This can be tricky to figure out for servings; here is how I proportion it out for the day: 1/3 loaf for breakfast, 1/3 loaf for lunch (including salad and veggies), 1/3 loaf for a snack or dessert after dinner. This recipe meets all required IP protein packets for a day.

# CHOCOLATE PEANUT BUTTER BOMBS

**Ingredients:**
1 IP milk or dark chocolate pudding mix (dry)
1 IP chocolate chip pancake mix (dry)
1 tsp. baking powder
1/3 C. liquid egg whites
1 tsp. olive oil
1 tsp *peanut butter cup flavor extract (or vanilla extract)
1 T. water
1 T. Walden Farms peanut butter
1 T. Walden Farms chocolate syrup
1 IP peanut butter protein bar
Cooking spray

**Directions:**
1. Preheat oven to 350 degrees.
2. Cut peanut butter protein bar in 6 pieces. Set aside.
3. In a medium bowl, mix dry ingredients. Add liquid ingredients; stir to mix. Batter will be thick.
4. Coat a regular size muffin tin with cooking spray. Add ½ the batter evenly into 6 muffin cups; place the peanut butter bar pieces into the

center of each cup pressing down into batter. Distribute the rest of the batter evenly on top of the peanut butter pieces.
5. Bake 10 - 15 minutes or until an inserted toothpick comes out clean. Insert into batter portion, not center where the bar is placed, to get an accurate reading.

**Servings:** 6 bombs = 2 unrestricted + 1 restricted

**TIP:** *You may purchase the peanut butter cup flavor extract from www.olivenation.com. Here is how I proportion out this recipe for the day: 2 for breakfast, 2 for lunch (including salad and veggies), 2 for a snack or dessert after dinner. This recipe meets all required IP protein packets for a day.

# CHOCOLATE ZUCCHINI MUFFINS

**Ingredients:**
1 IP dark chocolate pudding mix (dry)
1 IP apple or maple oatmeal mix (dry)
1 tsp. baking powder
1 tsp. sugar free sweetener, granular
¼ tsp. cinnamon
1/3 C. liquid egg whites
1 tsp. olive oil
1 T. milk
2 T. water
½ C. shredded zucchini
Cooking spray

**Directions:**
1. Preheat oven to 350 degrees.
2. Place shredded zucchini in a microwave safe bowl and cook on high for 1 minute; remove from microwave and blot with paper towels to absorb moisture. Set

aside.
3.  In a medium bowl, mix together the dry ingredients.
4.  Add liquid ingredients.  Stir to mix; batter will be thick.  Fold in shredded zucchini.
5.  Coat a regular size muffin tin with cooking spray; spoon batter into 6 muffin tins.
6.  Bake 15 - 17 minutes.

**Servings:**  6 muffins = 2 unrestricted servings + ½ C. veggies;  3 muffins = 1 unrestricted + ¼ C. veggies

## CHUNKY PEANUT BUTTER MUFFINS

**Ingredients:**
1 IP peanut butter soy puffs, slightly crushed (not to crumbs)
1 IP plain pancake mix (dry)
1 tsp. baking powder
1/3 C. liquid egg whites
2 T. Walden Farms peanut butter spread
1 T. water
Cooking spray

**Directions:**
1. Preheat oven to 350 degrees.
2. In a medium bowl, mix the dry ingredients.
3. Add the remaining ingredients; stir to mix.
4. Spray a jumbo muffin tin (Texas size) with cooking spray and spoon batter into muffin tin making 2 jumbo muffins.  If you do not have a Texas size muffin tin, see TIP below.
5. Bake 10 - 12 minutes; or until an inserted toothpick comes out clean.

**Servings:**  2 muffins = 1 unrestricted + 1 restricted; 1 muffin = ½ unrestricted + ½ restricted

**TIP:**  If eating one muffin as a meal in one day, I would count this as a restricted for that day (even though it's ½ restricted + ½ unrestricted). If you do not have a Texas size muffin tin, use a regular size muffin tin making 6 muffins, bake 8 – 10 minutes.  Eat 3 muffins for same serving equivalent to 1 jumbo muffin.

## CHURRO BREAD

**Ingredients:**
1 IP vanilla pudding mix (dry)
1 IP plain pancake mix (dry)
1 tsp. baking powder
1 tsp. sugar free sweetener, granular
1 tsp. cinnamon
½ tsp. nutmeg
1 egg
2 T. liquid egg whites
2 tsp. olive oil
1 T. water
2 T. milk
Cooking spray

**Directions:**
1.  Preheat oven to 350 degrees.
2.  In a medium mixing bowl, mix together the dry ingredients.
3.  Add liquid ingredients and stir to mix.
4.  Pour batter into sprayed 5 3/8" x 3" x 2 1/8" mini loaf pan.
5.  Bake 17 - 19 minutes or until inserted toothpick comes out clean.
6.  Cool completely; excellent when sliced and toasted.

**Servings:**  Entire loaf = 2 unrestricted + 2 oz. lean protein; ½ loaf = 1 unrestricted + 1 oz. lean protein

## CINNAMON & SUGAR TOAST

**Ingredients:**
1 IP crispy cereal mix (dry), crushed
¼ tsp. baking powder
1/8 tsp. cinnamon
1 tsp. sugar free sweetener, granular
½ tsp. olive oil
1/3 C. liquid egg whites
¼ tsp. vanilla extract
Cooking spray
Walden Farms fruit spread or syrup, for topping

**Directions:**
1.  Preheat oven to 350 degrees.
2.  In a medium bowl, mix dry ingredients together; add liquid ingredients and stir to mix.
3.  Coat a 5" x 5" square pan with cooking spray (a standard size rectangular loaf pan may be used.) Pour batter into sprayed pan.
4.  Bake 12 - 14 minutes.
5.  Cool completely - this will help the texture be more like toast.
6.  Place in toaster until crisp and browned.
7.  Serve with Walden Farms fruit spread or syrup for dipping.

**Servings:**  1 unrestricted

## CINNAMON MAPLE MUFFINS

**Ingredients:**
1 IP maple oatmeal mix (dry)
1 IP crispy cereal (dry), crushed
2 tsp. baking powder
1/3 C. liquid egg whites
1 T. milk
2 tsp. olive oil
½ tsp. vanilla extract
½ tsp. sugar free sweetener, granular
½ tsp. cinnamon
2 tsp. Walden Farms pancake syrup
¼ C. IP vanilla pre-made drink
Cooking spray

**Directions:**
1.  Preheat oven to 350 degrees.
2.  In a medium bowl, mix together the dry ingredients.
3.  Add liquid ingredients; stir to mix.
4.  Spray a regular size muffin tin with cooking spray.  Pour batter into muffin tins making 4 muffins.
5.  Bake 10-12 minutes.

**Servings:**  4 muffins = 2 unrestricted; 2 muffins = 1 unrestricted

## CINNAVANILLA LOAF BREAD

**Ingredients:**
1 IP vanilla pudding mix (dry)
1 IP plain pancake mix (dry)
1 tsp. baking powder
1 tsp. cinnamon

1/3 C. liquid egg whites
2 T. water
1 T. Walden Farms caramel syrup
1 T. Walden Farms pancake syrup
Cooking spray

**Directions:**
1. Preheat oven to 350 degrees.
2. In a medium bowl, mix together the dry ingredients.
3. Add liquid ingredients; stir to mix.
4. Spray a 5 3/8" x 3" x 2 1/8" mini loaf pan with cooking spray and add batter. Smooth down the batter with the back of a sprayed spoon to even out.
5. Bake 20 minutes or until an inserted toothpick comes out clean.

**Servings:** Entire loaf = 2 unrestricted; ½ loaf = 1 unrestricted

## CORNBREAD BISCUITS
*Nacho cheese or Sweet chili*

**Ingredients:**
1 packet IP Dorados, any flavor
1 IP potato puree (dry)
1 tsp. baking powder
1 egg
2 T. water
½ C. shredded zucchini
Cooking spray

**Directions:**
1. Preheat oven to 350 degrees.
2. Place zucchini in a small microwave proof bowl and microwave on high 1 minute. Blot with paper towels to absorb excess moisture; set aside.
3. Place Dorados, potato puree and baking powder in a bullet blender; blend to crumbs.
4. In a medium mixing bowl, whisk together egg, water and zucchini. Add Dorado mixture; stir to mix.
5. Spray a 12 cavity brownie pan making 4 biscuits (or, you may use a standard size muffin tin making 4

muffins).
6. Bake 10 – 12 minutes or until inserted toothpick comes out clean.
7. Cool biscuits on cooling rack; cut in half and toast lightly in toaster.

**Servings:** 4 biscuits = 2 unrestricted + 2 oz. lean protein + ½ C. veggies; 2 biscuits = 1 unrestricted + 1 oz. lean protein + ¼ C. veggies

## CRANBERRY ORANGE MUFFINS

**Ingredients:**
1 IP plain pancake mix (dry)
½ tsp. baking powder
2 T. liquid egg whites
1 T. water
1 T. Walden Farms orange marmalade spread
1 T. Walden Farms cranberry spread
Cooking spray

**Directions:**
1. Preheat oven to 350 degrees.
2. In a medium bowl, mix dry ingredients.
3 Add the liquid egg whites and water; stir to mix.
4. Place the cranberry spread and orange marmalade in a small bowl; microwave on high 15 seconds. Slowly add to the muffin batter, stirring to incorporate.
5. Spray regular size muffin tin with cooking spray; spoon batter into muffin tin making three muffins.
6. Bake 10 minutes.

**Servings:** 3 muffins = 1 unrestricted

## CRÈME BRULEE MUFFIN BREAD

**Ingredients:**
1 IP vanilla pudding mix (dry)
1 IP plain pancake mix (dry)
1 tsp. baking powder
1 tsp. sugar free sweetener, granular
¼ tsp. cinnamon
1/3 C. liquid egg whites
2 tsp. olive oil
1 T. water
1 T. milk (or IP vanilla

pre-made drink)
2 tsp. *Grand Marnier emulsion
Cooking spray

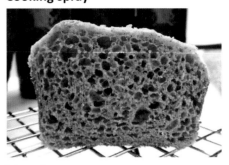

**Directions:**
1. Preheat oven to 350 degrees.
2. In a medium mixing bowl, mix together the dry ingredients; add liquid ingredients and stir to mix.
3. Pour batter into sprayed 5 3/8" x 3" x 2 1/8" mini loaf pan.
4. Bake 17 - 19 minutes or until inserted toothpick comes out clean.

**Servings:** Entire loaf = 2 unrestricted; ½ loaf = 1 unrestricted

**TIP:** *You may purchase Grand Marnier emulsion at www.olivenation.com. In this recipe 1 tsp. orange extract + 1 tsp. vanilla extract may be substituted for the Grand Marnier flavored emulsion to get a similar flavor. This makes great French Toast, pg. 63.

## DARK CHOCOLATE OATMEAL BREAD

**Ingredients:**
1 IP dark chocolate pudding mix (dry)
1 IP maple oatmeal mix (dry)
2 tsp. baking powder
½ tsp. vanilla extract
1/3 C. liquid egg whites
1 tsp. olive oil
2 T. Walden Farms chocolate syrup
¼ C. water or milk
Cooking spray

**Directions:**
1. Preheat oven to 350 degrees.
2. In a medium sized mixing bowl, mix together the dry ingredients. Add the liquid ingredients; stir to mix.
3. Spray a 5 3/8" x 3" x 2 1/8" mini loaf pan with cooking spray and add batter. Lightly pat down with the back of a sprayed spoon to even out.
4. Bake for 23 - 26 minutes or until inserted toothpick comes out clean.

**Servings:** Entire loaf = 2 unrestricted; ½ loaf = 1 unrestricted

# DOUBLE CHOCOLATE CHIP MUFFINS

*A favorite recipe for chocolate lovers*

**Ingredients:**
1 IP dark chocolate pudding mix (dry)
1 IP chocolate chip pancake mix (dry)
1 tsp. baking powder
1 tsp. sugar free sweetener, granular
1/3 C. liquid egg whites
2 tsp. olive oil
4 T. water
Cooking spray

**Directions:**
1. Preheat oven to 350 degrees.
2. In a medium bowl, mix together the dry ingredients.
3. Add liquid ingredients; stir to mix.
4. Spray a regular size muffin tin with cooking spray; spoon batter into muffin tin making 6 muffins.
5. Bake 10 - 12 minutes.

**Servings:** 6 muffins = 2 unrestricted; 3 muffins = 1 unrestricted

# FROST ON THE PUMPKIN PIE MUFFIN BREAD

*Inspired by a Frost on the Pumpkin Pie my mother always makes for the holidays*

**Ingredients:** (muffin bread)
1 IP vanilla pudding mix (dry)
1 IP plain pancake mix (dry)
1 tsp. baking powder
1 tsp. sugar free sweetener, granular
2 tsp. pumpkin pie spice
2 tsp. olive oil
3 T. Walden Farms caramel syrup
1 T. milk
1/3 C. liquid egg whites
Cooking spray

**Directions:**
1. Preheat oven to 350 degrees.
2. In a medium bowl, mix together the dry ingredients.
3. Add liquid ingredients; stir to mix.
4. Spray a 5 3/8" x 3" x 2 1/8" mini loaf pan; add batter and lightly pat down with the back of a sprayed spoon so batter is even.
5. Bake 20 - 22 minutes or until inserted toothpick comes out clean. Cool.

**Ingredients:** (cinnamon frosting)
2 T. Walden Farms marshmallow dip
1 tsp. Walden Farms caramel dip (or pancake syrup or caramel syrup)
¼ tsp. cinnamon

**Directions:**
1. Mix ingredients together in a small bowl and spread on cooled Frost on the Pumpkin Pie Muffin Bread. Slice to serve.

**Servings:** Entire loaf with frosting = 2 unrestricted; ½ loaf with frosting = 1 unrestricted

# GARLIC ROASTED TOMATO ROLLS

**Ingredients:**
1 IP potato puree mix (dry)
1 IP crispy cereal mix (dry), crushed
2 tsp. baking powder

Pinch of IP salt
1/3 C. liquid egg whites
¼ C. (2 oz.) milk
1 tsp. olive oil
¼ C. Garlic Roasted Tomatoes, pg. 91
Cooking spray

**Directions:**
1. Preheat oven to 350 degrees.
2. In a medium mixing bowl, mix together the dry ingredients with a whisk.
3. Add liquid ingredients and stir until mixed; fold tomatoes into batter.
4. Scoop batter into a sprayed regular size muffin tin making 6 rolls.
5. Bake 10 - 12 minutes or until inserted toothpick comes out clean.

**Servings:** 6 rolls = 2 unrestricted + ½ C. veggies; 3 rolls = 1 unrestricted + ¼ C. veggies.

**TIP:** These are delicious when cut in half and toasted in the toaster.

# GARLIC ZUCCHINI BAGELS

**Ingredients:**
1 IP potato puree mix (dry)
1 IP crispy cereal mix (dry), crushed
2 tsp. baking powder
½ tsp. garlic powder
Pinch of salt
1/3 C. liquid egg whites
1/4 C. (2 oz.) milk
1 tsp. olive oil
½ C. shredded zucchini
Cooking spray

## Directions:

1. Preheat oven to 350 degrees.
2. Place shredded zucchini in a small bowl; microwave on high 1 minute.
3. Blot with paper towels to remove excess moisture; set aside.
4. In a medium bowl, mix together the dry ingredients.
5. Add liquid ingredients; stir to mix. Fold in zucchini.
6. Scoop batter into a sprayed regular size donut pan making 4 bagels.
7. Bake 12-14 minutes or until inserted toothpick comes out clean.

**Servings:** 4 bagels = 2 unrestricted; 2 bagels = 1 unrestricted

**TIP:** These bagels make great sandwich or burger buns.

## GINGERBREAD

Ingredients:
1 IP vanilla pudding mix (dry)
1 IP plain pancake mix (dry)
½ tsp. cinnamon
1/8 tsp. ground cloves
1/8 tsp. ginger
1/8 tsp. nutmeg
1 tsp. baking powder
1 tsp. sugar free sweetener, granular (optional)
1/3 C. liquid egg whites
2 tsp. olive oil
3 T. Walden Farms caramel syrup
1 T. water
½ tsp. *pumpkin pie or butterscotch flavor fountain extract, optional
Cooking spray
Glaze (for topping), pg. 42

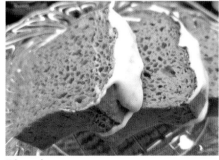

## Directions:

1. Preheat oven to 350 degrees.
3. In a medium mixing bowl, add dry ingredients; stir to mix.
4. Add liquid ingredients; stir to mix.
5. Spray a 5 3/8" x 3" x 2 1/8" mini loaf pan with cooking spray; pour

batter into pan.
6. Bake 23-25 minutes or until an inserted toothpick comes out clean.
7. Cool loaf and drizzle with glaze (optional).

**Servings:** Entire loaf = 2 unrestricted; 1/2 loaf = 1 unrestricted

**TIP:** *You may purchase the pumpkin pie and/or butterscotch flavor fountain at www.olivenation.com. It is optional but adds great flavor, color and texture to this bread; I highly recommend it.

## GLAZED CINNAMON ROLLS

Ingredients:
1 IP vanilla pudding mix (dry)
1 IP plain pancake mix (dry)
1 tsp. baking powder
1 tsp. sugar free sweetener, granular
1/3 C. liquid egg whites
2 tsp. olive oil
4 T. water
¼ tsp. cinnamon
Cooking spray
Glaze (for topping), pg. 42

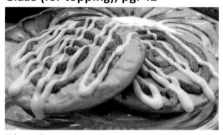

## Directions:

1. Preheat oven to 350 degrees.
2. In a medium bowl, mix together the dry ingredients (except cinnamon).
3. Add liquid ingredients; stir to mix.
4. Place approximately 1/6 of the batter into a separate bowl. Add the cinnamon; stir to mix.
5. Spray a muffin top tin with cooking spray; spoon plain vanilla batter into muffin top tin making 4 cinnamon rolls. If you don't have a muffin top pan, see TIP below.
6. Place the cinnamon batter into one corner of a sandwich baggie making a piping bag. Clip ¼ " off the plastic baggie corner and squeeze the cinnamon batter onto the

cinnamon buns in a circular pattern.
7. Bake 8 minutes or until done; drizzle with glaze.

**Servings:** 4 rolls = 2 unrestricted; 2 rolls = 1 unrestricted

**TIP:** If you don't have a muffin top tin, make 4 three inch rounds on a parchment lined baking sheet.

## GLAZED LEMON ZUCCHINI SCONES

Ingredients: (scones)
1 IP vanilla pudding mix (dry)
1 IP plain pancake mix (dry)
1 tsp. baking powder
1 tsp. sugar free sweetener, granular
1/3 C. liquid egg whites
1 whole egg, slightly beaten
1 tsp. lemon extract
2 tsp. olive oil
1 T. water
4 drops yellow food coloring, optional
½ C. shredded zucchini
Cooking spray

## Directions:

1. Preheat oven to 350 degrees.
2. Place zucchini in a small bowl; microwave on high 1 minute. Blot zucchini with a paper towel to absorb as much moisture as possible; set aside to cool.
3. In a medium bowl, mix together the dry ingredients.
4. In a separate medium bowl, whisk together liquid ingredients including zucchini.
5. Add dry ingredients and stir to mix.
6. Fill a sprayed 6 cavity scone pan making 6 scones; bake 6 minutes or until an inserted toothpick comes out clean. (NOTE: If you do not have a scone pan, pour batter into a

sprayed 8" round baking pan; bake 8-10 minutes or until an inserted toothpick comes out clean. Slice into 6 pie shaped pieces.)
7. Cool completely and drizzle with lemon glaze (recipe to follow).

**Ingredients:** (lemon glaze)
2 T. Walden Farms marshmallow dip
2 tsp. Walden Farms pancake syrup
½ tsp. lemon juice

**Directions:**
1. Place glaze ingredients in a small bowl and vigorously whisk with a fork or whisk until blended; frost or drizzle over cooled scones.

**Servings:** 6 scones = 2 unrestricted + 2 oz. lean protein (whole egg) + ½ C. veggies; 3 scones = 1 unrestricted + 1 oz. lean protein + ¼ C. veggies

**TIP:** It is important to cool scones completely or the texture will be spongy; once cooled, they are moist and delicious. Texture will be more muffin-like than scone-like, yet will take on the look and shape of a scone to add variety and interest to your meals. Excellent when lightly toasted in the toaster.

## INDIAN CURRY NAAN BREAD

**Ingredients:**
1 IP potato puree mix (dry)
¼ tsp. baking powder
½ tsp. yellow curry spice
1/3 C. liquid egg whites
1 tsp. olive oil
Cooking spray

**Directions:**
1. In a small bowl, mix together all dry ingredients. Add liquid ingredients; stir to blend.
2. Heat a small frying pan over medium heat; spray with cooking spray. Add batter and spread into a

large pancake size with the back of a sprayed spoon.
3. Cook until browned, flip and cook the other side.

**Servings:** 1 unrestricted

## LEMON CHOCOLATE CHIP MINI MUFFINS

**Ingredients:**
1 IP vanilla pudding mix (dry)
1 IP chocolate chip pancake mix (dry)
1 tsp. baking powder
1 tsp. sugar free sweetener, granular
1/3 C. liquid egg whites
2 tsp. olive oil
4 T. water
½ tsp. lemon extract
Cooking spray

**Directions:**
1. Preheat oven to 350 degrees.
2. In a medium bowl, mix together the dry ingredients.
3. Add liquid ingredients; stir to mix.
4. Spray a mini muffin tin with cooking spray; spoon batter into muffin tin making 12 muffins.
5. Bake 8 - 10 minutes.

**Servings:** 12 mini muffins = 2 unrestricted; 6 mini muffins = 1 unrestricted

## LEMON CHOCOLATE WAFER BREAD

**Ingredients:**
1 IP vanilla pudding mix (dry)
1 IP crispy cereal mix (dry), crushed
2 tsp. baking powder
¼ tsp. sugar free sweetener, granular
1/3 C. liquid egg whites
½ tsp. lemon extract
1 tsp. olive oil
1 T. milk
¼ C. IP vanilla pre-made drink
1 IP lemon wafer bar (2 squares), cut in chunks
Cooking spray

**Directions:**
1. Preheat oven to 350 degrees.
2. In a medium bowl, mix together the dry ingredients except lemon wafer bars.
3. Add liquid ingredients; stir to mix.
4. Cut lemon wafer bars in chunks; fold into batter.
5. Spray a 5 3/8" x 3" x 2 1/8" mini loaf pan with cooking spray; even out the batter with the back of a sprayed spoon.
6. Bake 22 - 26 minutes or until an inserted toothpick comes clean.

**Servings:** Entire loaf = 3 unrestricted; 1/3 loaf = 1 unrestricted

## MUSHROOM PITA BREAD

**Ingredients:**
1 IP mushroom soup mix (dry)
¼ tsp. baking powder
Onion powder, to taste
1/3 C. liquid egg whites
1 tsp. olive oil
Cooking spray

**Directions:**
1. In a bowl, blend dry ingredients. Add liquid ingredients; mix well.
2. Spray an 8-inch frying pan with cooking spray and heat on medium heat. Spread mixture in pan. Batter will be thick; spread it into a 6"+ circle with the back of a sprayed spoon.
3. Cook until edges look dry and bottom of pita is browned, approximately 2 minutes; flip and continue cooking for 30 seconds or until browned.

**Servings:** 1 unrestricted

**TIP:** Stuff with veggies and/or meat and fold; for a variation, make two separate round buns.

## ORANGE CHOCOLATE CHIP ZUCCHINI MUFFINS

**Ingredients:**
1 IP chocolate chip pancake mix (dry)
¼ tsp. baking powder
2 T. liquid egg whites
2 T. Walden Farms chocolate syrup
¼ C. shredded zucchini
¼ tsp. orange extract, sugar free
Cooking spray

**Directions:**
1. Preheat oven to 350 degrees.
2. In a small microwave-proof bowl, microwave shredded zucchini on high for one minute; blot with paper towels to absorb moisture. Set aside.
3. In a medium bowl, mix dry ingredients.
4. Add the liquid ingredients; stir to mix. Fold in shredded zucchini.
5. Spray a regular size muffin tin with cooking spray; spoon batter into muffin tin making 3 muffins.
6. Bake 10 minutes.

**Servings:** 1 unrestricted + ¼ C. veggies

## PEANUT BUTTER & JELLY MUFFIN BREAD

**Ingredients:**
1 IP vanilla pudding mix (dry)
1 IP crispy cereal (dry), crushed
2 tsp. baking powder
1 tsp. sugar free sweetener, granular
Pinch of IP salt
1/3 C. liquid egg whites
1 tsp. olive oil
1 T. milk

2 T. IP vanilla pre-made drink
2 T. Walden Farms peanut butter
Cooking spray
Walden Farms grape spread (for topping)

**Directions:**
1. Preheat oven to 350 degrees.
2. In a medium bowl, mix together the dry ingredients.
3. Add liquid ingredients; stir to mix.
4. Spray a 5 3/8" x 3" x 2 1/8" mini loaf pan with cooking spray and add batter. Lightly pat down with the back of a sprayed spoon to even out the batter.
5. Bake for 20 - 25 minutes or until inserted toothpick comes out clean.
6. Serve topped with warmed Walden Farms grape spread.

**Servings:** Entire loaf = 2 unrestricted; ½ loaf = 1 unrestricted

## PEANUT BUTTER & JELLY TOAST

**Ingredients:**
1 IP crispy cereal mix (dry), crushed
¼ tsp. baking powder
1 tsp. sugar free sweetener, granular
½ tsp. olive oil
2 T. liquid egg whites
1 T. Walden Farms peanut butter
1 tsp. *peanut butter flavor extract (or 1 tsp. Walden Farms peanut butter)
Cooking spray
Walden Farms fruit spread (any flavor)

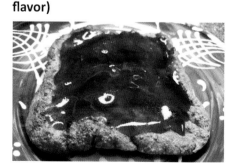

**Directions:**
1. Preheat oven to 350 degrees.
2. In a medium bowl, mix all dry

ingredients.
3. Add liquid ingredients; stir to mix.
4. Spray a 5"x 5" square baking pan (or standard loaf pan). Pour batter into the pan; spread batter evenly with the back of a sprayed spoon.
5. Bake 10 - 12 minutes or until center is done.
6. Place the bread slice in the toaster until crisp and browned.
7. Serve with warmed Walden Farms fruit spread.

**Servings:** 1 unrestricted

**TIP:** *You may purchase the peanut butter flavor extract online at www.olivenation.com.

## PEANUT BUTTER CUP MUFFINS

**Ingredients:**
1 IP chocolate chip pancake mix (dry)
½ tsp. baking powder
2 T. liquid egg whites
1 T. Walden Farms peanut butter
1 T. Walden Farms chocolate syrup
Cooking spray

**Directions:**
1. Preheat oven to 350 degrees.
2. In a medium bowl mix together the dry ingredients.
3. Add the liquid ingredients. Stir to mix.
4. Spray a regular size muffin tin with cooking spray; spoon batter into muffin tin making 3 muffins.
5. Bake 10 minutes.

**Servings:** 1 unrestricted

# POTATO BISCUITS

**Ingredients:**
1 IP potato puree mix (dry)
1 IP crispy cereal mix (dry), crushed
2 tsp. baking powder
¼ tsp. garlic powder
¼ tsp. onion powder
Pinch of IP salt
1/3 C. liquid egg whites
¼ C. (2 oz.) milk
1 tsp. olive oil
Cooking spray

**Directions:**
1. Preheat oven to 350 degrees.
2. In a medium mixing bowl, mix together the dry ingredients.
3. Add liquid ingredients and stir to mix.
4. Scoop batter into a sprayed regular size muffin tin making 6 biscuits.
5. Bake 10 - 12 minutes or until inserted toothpick comes out clean.

**Servings:** 6 biscuits = 2 unrestricted; 3 biscuits = 1 unrestricted

# POTATO PANCAKE BUNS

**Ingredients:**
1 IP plain pancake mix (dry)
1 IP potato puree mix (dry)
½ tsp. baking powder
Pinch of IP salt
¼ tsp. garlic powder
¼ tsp. onion powder
2 tsp. olive oil
2 T. milk
½ C. water
Cooking spray

**Directions:**
1. Preheat oven to 350 degrees; the pancake buns will first be cooked in a skillet and then baked.
2. In a medium bowl, mix together the dry ingredients.
3. Add liquid ingredients; stir to mix.
4. Heat a large skillet over medium/medium low heat and coat with cooking spray.
5. Divide batter, making 4 pancakes the size of hamburger buns.
6. Cook approximately 1 ½ - 2 minutes or until browned. Flip pancakes and cook other sides approximately 30 seconds or until browned.
7. Place the pancakes on a baking sheet and bake for 5 minutes.

**Servings:** 4 pancakes = 2 unrestricted; 2 pancakes = 1 unrestricted

**TIP:** These buns are great with fried or poached eggs as a breakfast sandwich; I also use them with the BBQ Sloppy Joe recipe.

# POTATO PITA BREAD WRAP

**Ingredients:**
1 IP potato puree mix (dry)
¼ tsp. baking powder
¼ tsp. Italian seasoning
¼ tsp. garlic powder
1/3 C. liquid egg whites
1 tsp. olive oil
Cooking spray

**Directions:**
1. In a bowl, blend dry ingredients. Add liquid ingredients; mix well.
2. Spray an 8-inch frying pan with cooking spray and heat on medium heat. Spread mixture in pan. Batter will be thick; spread it into a 6"+ circle with the back of a sprayed spoon.
3. Cook until edges look dry and bottom of pita is browned, approximately 2 minutes; flip and continue cooking for 30 seconds or until browned.

**Servings:** 1 unrestricted

**TIP:** Stuff with veggies and/or meat and fold; for a variation, make two separate round buns.

# POTATO PUREE WAFFLE BUNS

*These buns are perfect for burgers or French dip au jus sandwiches*

**Ingredients:**
1 IP potato puree mix (dry)
¼ tsp. baking powder
¼ tsp. garlic powder
3 T. liquid egg whites
1 T. milk
Cooking spray

**Directions:**
1. In a medium bowl, mix together the dry ingredients.
2. Add liquid ingredients; stir to mix. Batter will be thick.
3. Preheat waffle maker and coat with cooking spray; add batter and bake 2 waffles according to waffle iron manufacturer directions.

**Servings:** 2 waffle buns = 1 unrestricted

# PUMPKIN BREAD

**Ingredients:**
1 IP vanilla pudding mix (dry)
1 IP maple oatmeal mix (dry)
2 tsp. baking powder
½ tsp. pumpkin pie spice
1/3 C. liquid egg whites
1 T. milk
2 tsp. olive oil
2 T. Walden Farms caramel syrup
¼ C. vanilla pre-made drink
½ tsp. *pumpkin pie flavor fountain, optional
Cooking spray

**Directions:**
1. Preheat oven to 350 degrees.
2. In a medium bowl, mix dry ingredients together. Add liquid ingredients; stir to mix.
3. Spray a 5 3/8" x 3" x 2 1/8" mini loaf pan with cooking spray and add batter. Lightly pat down with the

back of a sprayed spoon to even out.
4. Bake 22 - 24 minutes or until an inserted toothpick comes out clean.

**Servings:** Entire recipe = 2 unrestricted; ½ recipe = 1 unrestricted

**TIP:** Slice and toast lightly in the toaster. Also makes excellent French toast, pg. 63. *Pumpkin Pie flavor fountain may be purchased at www.olivenation.com.

## PUMPKIN ZUCCHINI MUFFINS

**Ingredients:**
1 IP vanilla pudding mix (dry)
1 IP plain pancake mix (dry)
1 tsp. pumpkin pie spice
1 tsp. baking powder
1 tsp. sugar free sweetener, granular
1/3 C. liquid egg whites
2 tsp. olive oil
2 T. water
1 T. Walden Farms caramel syrup
½ C. shredded zucchini
Cooking spray

**Directions:**
1. Preheat oven to 350 degrees.
2. Microwave shredded zucchini on high for 1 minute. Blot with paper towels to absorb excess moisture; set aside.
3. In a medium bowl, mix together the dry ingredients.
4. Add liquid ingredients; stir to mix. Fold in zucchini.
5. Spray a regular size muffin tin with cooking spray; spoon batter into

muffin tin making 6 muffins.
6. Bake 12 minutes or until inserted toothpick comes clean.

**Servings:** 6 muffins = 2 unrestricted + 1/2 C. veggies; 3 muffins = 1 unrestricted + 1/4 C. veggies

## RASPBERRY CHOCOLATE CHIP MUFFINS

**Ingredients:**
1 IP chocolate chip pancake mix (dry)
¼ tsp. baking powder
2 T. liquid egg whites
2 T. Walden Farms raspberry spread
Cooking spray

**Directions:**
1. Preheat oven to 350 degrees.
2. Place the pancake mix in a medium bowl; add baking powder and stir to incorporate. Set aside.
3. Place the raspberry spread in a separate small bowl. Microwave on high for 15 seconds; stir.
4. Add liquid egg whites to the pancake mixture, stirring gently just to cover egg whites with mix; slowly pour in the raspberry spread, stirring continuously so the heated raspberry spread does not pre-cook the egg whites. Continue to stir until fully mixed.
5. Spray a regular size muffin tin with cooking spray; spoon batter evenly into muffin tin making 3 muffins.
6. Bake 10 minutes.

**Servings:** 3 muffins = 1 unrestricted

## S'MORES MUFFINS

**Ingredients:**
1 IP vanilla pudding mix (dry)
1 IP chocolate chip pancake mix (dry)
1 tsp. baking powder
1/3 C. liquid egg whites
1 tsp. olive oil
1 T. Walden Farms marshmallow dip
1 T. Walden Farms chocolate syrup
Cooking Spray

**Directions:**
1. Preheat oven to 350 degrees.
2. In a medium bowl, mix together the dry ingredients.
3. Add liquid ingredients; stir to mix.
4. Spray a regular size muffin tin with cooking spray; spoon batter into muffin tins making 6 muffins.
5. Bake 8-10 minutes or until an inserted toothpick comes out clean.

**Servings:** 6 muffins = 2 unrestricted; 3 muffins = 1 unrestricted

## SNICKERDOODLE MUFFINS

**Ingredients:** (muffins)
1 IP vanilla pudding mix (dry)
1 IP plain pancake mix (dry)
1 tsp. baking powder
1 tsp. cinnamon
1/3 C. liquid egg whites
1 tsp. vanilla extract
2 tsp. olive oil
4 T. water
Cooking spray

**Ingredients:** (cinnamon & sugar topping)
1 ½ tsp. sugar free sweetener, granular
¼ - ½ tsp. cinnamon

**Directions:**
1. Preheat oven to 350 degrees.
2. In a medium bowl, mix together the dry ingredients for the muffins.
3. In a separate small bowl mix together the cinnamon and sugar topping ingredients.
4. Add liquid ingredients to the dry muffin ingredients; stir to mix.
5. Spray a regular size muffin tin with cooking spray; spoon batter into muffin tin making 4 muffins.
6. Bake 2 ½ minutes; remove from oven and sprinkle muffins with the cinnamon and sugar topping. Place back in the oven.
7. Bake 10 minutes or until an inserted toothpick comes out clean.

**Servings:** 4 muffins = 2 unrestricted; 2 muffins = 1 unrestricted

## STRAWBERRY CHEESECAKE CHOCOLATE CHIP MUFFINS

**Ingredients:**
1 IP vanilla pudding mix (dry)
1 IP chocolate chip pancake mix (dry)
1 tsp. baking powder
1 tsp. sugar free sweetener, granular
1/3 C. liquid egg whites
2 tsp. olive oil
2 tsp. *cream cheese emulsion
3 T. Walden Farms strawberry syrup
Cooking spray

**Directions:**
1. Preheat oven to 350 degrees.
2. In a medium bowl, mix together the dry ingredients.
3. Add liquid ingredients; stir to mix.
4. Spray a mini muffin tin with cooking spray; spoon batter into muffin tin making 12 muffins.
5. Bake 10 minutes.

**Servings:** 12 mini muffins = 2 unrestricted; 6 mini muffins = 1 unrestricted

**TIP:** *You may purchase the cream cheese emulsion from www.olivenation.com.

## STRAWBERRY RHUBARB OATMEAL MUFFINS

**Ingredients:**
3 tsp. Strawberry Rhubarb Compote, pg. 45
1 IP maple or apple oatmeal mix (dry)
1 tsp. baking powder
¼ tsp. cinnamon
2 T. liquid egg whites
2 T. Walden Farms pancake syrup
Cooking spray

**Directions:**
1. Preheat oven to 350 degrees.
2. In a medium bowl, mix dry ingredients. Add liquid ingredients; stir to mix.
3. Spray a regular size muffin tin with cooking spray; spoon batter into muffin tin making 3 muffins.
4. Top each muffin with 1 tsp. Strawberry Rhubarb Compote.
5. Bake 10 minutes.

**Servings:** 1 unrestricted + 3 tsp. veggies

## STRAWBERRY RHUBARB UPSIDE-DOWN MUFFINS

**Ingredients:**
3 tsp. Strawberry Rhubarb Compote, pg. 45
1 IP plain pancake mix (dry)
¼ tsp. baking powder
2 T. liquid egg whites
2 T. Walden Farms strawberry syrup
Cooking spray

**Directions:**
1. Preheat oven to 350 degrees.
2. In a medium bowl, mix dry ingredients. Add liquid ingredients;

stir to mix.
3. Spray a regular size muffin tin with cooking spray; spoon batter into muffin tin making 3 muffins.
4. Top each muffin with 1 tsp. Strawberry Rhubarb Compote.
5. Bake 10 minutes.
6. Cool muffins upside-down (rhubarb mixture will sink to the bottom during baking).

**Servings:** 1 unrestricted + 3 tsp. veggies

## TEXAS TURTLE MUFFIN
*Caramel, Chocolate and Pecan Flavors*

**Ingredients:** (muffin)
1 IP chocolatey caramel mug cake mix (dry)
1/2 tsp. baking powder
¼ tsp. cinnamon
3 T. liquid egg whites
1 tsp. olive oil
1 tsp. *pecan flavor extract (or vanilla extract)
1 T. Walden Farms caramel syrup
1 T. milk
Cooking spray

**Ingredients:** (drizzle)
Walden Farms chocolate syrup, to taste
Walden Farms caramel syrup, to taste

**Directions:**
1. Preheat oven to 350 degrees.
2. In a medium bowl, mix together the dry ingredients.
3. Add liquid ingredients; stir to mix.
4. Spoon batter into a sprayed Texas muffin tin, making 1 muffin. (NOTE:

See tip below if you do not have a Texas sized muffin tin.)
5. Bake 16 - 18 minutes or until an inserted toothpick comes out clean.
6. Drizzle with Walden Farms syrups.

**Servings:** 1 jumbo muffin = 1 unrestricted

**TIP:** A Texas sized muffin tin makes jumbo sized muffins. If you do not have this pan size, use a regular muffin tin making 2 muffins; bake 10-12 minutes. Two regular size muffins = 1 unrestricted.
* You may purchase the pecan flavor extract at www.olivenation.com, adding to the classic turtle flavors.

## TOMATO BASIL LOAF BREAD
*Makes great slider buns*

**Ingredients:**
1 IP tomato basil soup (dry)
1 IP crispy cereal mix (dry), crushed
2 tsp. baking powder
¼ tsp Italian seasoning
¼ tsp. garlic powder
¼ tsp. crushed rosemary
1/8 tsp. onion powder
Pinch of IP salt
1/3 C. liquid egg whites
¼ C. milk
2 tsp. olive oil
Cooking spray

**Directions:**
1. Preheat oven to 350 degrees.
2. In a medium sized bowl, mix dry ingredients together.
3. Add liquid ingredients; stir to mix. Batter will be thick like cookie dough.
4. Spray a 5 3/8" x 3" x 2 1/8" mini loaf pan with cooking spray and add batter. Lightly pat down with the back of a sprayed spoon to even out.
5. Bake for 18 - 22 minutes or until inserted toothpick comes out clean. Slice and serve.

**Servings:** 1 mini loaf = 2 unrestricted; ½ mini loaf = 1 unrestricted

**TIP:** Great as a side with salad or soup. Toast slices lightly in toaster for slider buns.

## TOMATO BASIL PITA BREAD WRAP

**Ingredients:**
1 IP tomato basil soup mix (dry)
¼ tsp. baking powder
Italian seasoning, to taste
Garlic powder, to taste
1/3 C. liquid egg whites
1 tsp. olive oil
Cooking spray

**Directions:**
1. In a bowl, blend dry ingredients. Add liquid ingredients; mix well.
2. Spray an 8-inch frying pan with cooking spray and heat on medium heat. Spread mixture in pan. Batter will be thick; spread it into a 6"+ circle with the back of a sprayed spoon.
3. Cook until edges look dry and bottom of pita is browned, approximately 2 minutes; flip and continue cooking for 30 seconds or until browned.

**Servings:** 1 unrestricted

**TIP:** Stuff with veggies and/or meat and fold; for a variation, make two separate round buns.

## TORTILLA WRAP

**Ingredients:**
2 C. (7 oz.) cauliflower florets, riced
½ tsp. garlic powder
½ tsp. Taco Seasoning, pg. 52
1 egg, beaten

**Directions:**
1. Preheat oven to 450 degrees.
2. In food processor, pulse the 2 cups cauliflower florets until pieces are rice size. Cook in microwave on

high for 5 - 6 minutes or until softened and cooked.
3. Add garlic powder and taco seasoning. Mix and let cool a bit.
4. Add beaten egg, stirring while adding so the egg doesn't cook in the cauliflower mixture.
5. Line a baking sheet with parchment paper.
6. Divide mixture in half. Spread two circles of batter on parchment paper as thinly and evenly as possible.
7. Bake 15 minutes. Remove from oven; peel wraps off parchment and flip. Bake one more minute.

**Servings:** 2 C. veggies + 2 oz. lean protein (whole egg)

## TROPICAL TWIST MUFFINS
*A tasty blend of strawberry and pina colada*

**Ingredients:**
1 IP pina colada drink mix (dry)
1 IP apple oatmeal mix (dry)
1 tsp. baking powder
1/3 C. liquid egg whites
1 tsp. olive oil
1 T. water
2 T. Walden Farms strawberry syrup
1 T. milk
Cooking spray

**Directions:**
1. Preheat oven to 350 degrees.
2. In a medium bowl, mix together the dry ingredients.
3. Add liquid ingredients. Stir to mix.
4. Spray a regular size muffin tin with cooking spray; spoon batter into muffin tin making 6 muffins.
5. Bake 10 minutes.

**Servings:** 6 muffins = 2 unrestricted; 3 muffins = 1 unrestricted

## VANILLA CHOCOLATE CHIP MUFFINS

**Ingredients:**
1 IP vanilla pudding mix (dry)
1 IP chocolate chip pancake mix (dry)
1 tsp. baking powder
1 tsp. sugar free sweetener, granular
1/3 C. liquid egg whites
2 tsp. olive oil
½ tsp. vanilla extract
4 T. water
Cooking spray

**Directions:**
1. Preheat oven to 350 degrees.
2. In a medium bowl, mix together the dry ingredients.
3. Add liquid ingredients; stir to mix.
4. Spray a regular size muffin tin with cooking spray; spoon batter into muffin tin making 6 muffins.
5. Bake 10 - 12 minutes.

**Servings:** 6 muffins = 2 unrestricted; 3 muffins = 1 unrestricted

## WHITE CHEDDAR GARLIC BUNS

*Excellent for burgers or sandwiches*

**Ingredients:**
1 IP potato puree mix (dry)
1 IP white cheddar ridges
1 tsp. baking powder
¼ tsp. garlic powder
1/3 C. liquid egg whites
¼ C. (2 oz.) milk
2 tsp. olive oil
Cooking spray

**Directions:**
1. Preheat oven to 350 degrees.
2. Place dry ingredients in a bullet blender; blend to crumbs. Transfer to medium size mixing bowl.
3. Add liquid ingredients and stir to mix.
4. Scoop batter into a sprayed 6 cavity muffin top pan making 4 buns.
5. Bake 8 - 10 minutes or until inserted toothpick comes out clean. Cool completely.

**Servings:** 4 buns = 1 unrestricted + 1 restricted; 2 buns = ½ unrestricted + ½ restricted

**TIP:** I count 2 buns as 1 restricted IP packet for the day even though they are ½ restricted and ½ unrestricted. Refrigerate the remaining 2 buns for another serving, another day. These buns are excellent when toasted lightly in the toaster.

## WILDBERRY OATMEAL MUFFINS

**Ingredients:**
1 IP wildberry yogurt drink mix (dry)
1 IP apple or maple oatmeal mix (dry)
1 tsp. baking powder
1 tsp. sugar free sweetener, granular
1/3 C. liquid egg whites
2 tsp. olive oil
2 T. milk
1 T. water
¼ tsp. cinnamon
Cooking spray

**Directions:**
1. Preheat oven to 350 degrees.
2. In a medium bowl, mix together the dry ingredients.
3. Add liquid ingredients. Stir to mix; batter will be thick.
4. Spray a regular size muffin tin with cooking spray; spoon batter into muffin tin making 6 muffins.
5. Bake 10 - 12 minutes.

**Servings:** 6 muffins = 2 unrestricted; 3 muffins = 1 unrestricted

## ZUCCHINI BREAD

**Ingredients:**
1 IP vanilla pudding mix (dry)
1 IP plain pancake mix (dry)
1 tsp. cinnamon
1 tsp. baking powder
1 tsp. sugar free sweetener, granular
1/3 C. liquid egg whites
2 tsp. olive oil
1 T. water
1 T. Walden Farms caramel syrup
2/3 C. shredded zucchini
Cooking spray

**Directions:**
1. Preheat oven to 350 degrees.
2. In a small bowl, microwave shredded zucchini on high for 1 minute. Blot with paper towels to remove moisture. Set aside.
3. In a medium mixing bowl, mix together the dry ingredients. Add liquid ingredients; stir to mix. Fold in shredded zucchini.
4. Spray a 5 3/8" x 3" x 2 1/8" mini loaf pan with cooking spray and add batter. Lightly pat down with the back of a sprayed spoon to even out.
5. Bake 16-19 minutes or until inserted toothpick comes out clean.

**Servings:** Entire loaf
= 2 unrestricted + 2/3 C. veggies;
½ loaf = 1 unrestricted + 1/3 C. veggies

# Desserts, Cookies & Cakes

"Vegetables are a must on a diet. I suggest Caramel Fried Apples, Birthday Carrot Cake or Strawberry Rhubarb Cobbler." *Janeva Eickhoff*

**Caramel Apple Pie**
**Page 38**

**Caramel Vanilla Latte Cake**
**Page 39**

**Chocolatey Coconut Almond Brownies - Page 40**

**Granola Cookies**
**Page 42**

**Rhubard Dump Cake**
**Page 45**

**Bread Pudding**
**Page 37**

# 1 MINUTE CHOCOLATE FUDGE CAKE

**Ingredients:**
1 IP chocolate chip pancake mix (dry)
1 T. Walden Farms chocolate syrup
2 T. water
½ - 1 tsp. *Fudge Brownie flavor fountain (optional)

**Directions:**
1. Place ingredients in a standard size coffee mug; stir to mix.
2. Microwave 55 seconds on high; turn over onto a plate after baking. (You may need to run a knife around the edges of the cake to loosen from the mug; no need for cooking spray.)
3. Drizzle cake with additional warmed Walden Farms chocolate syrup.

**Servings:** 1 unrestricted

**TIP:** *You may purchase the Fudge Brownie flavor fountain from www.olivenation.com. It adds a tremendous amount of flavor and color but is not necessary for the cake to bake.

# AIRPLANE COOKIES
*Apple cinnamon spice flavor*

**Ingredients:**
1 package IP apple cinnamon soy puffs
1/8 tsp. baking powder
1 tsp. sugar free sweetener, granular
3 T. water
Cooking spray

**Directions:**
1. Preheat oven to 350 degrees.
2. Add dry ingredients to a blender or food processor; blend to fine crumbs.
3. Transfer to a small bowl; add water and mix.
4. Evenly drop 6 spoonfuls of batter onto a parchment lined baking sheet.
5. Spread into thin circles with the back of a spoon sprayed with cooking spray; you may also pat down with your fingers.
6. Bake 10 minutes; take out of oven and flip. Bake another 5 minutes.

**Servings:** 6 cookies = 1 restricted

**TIP:** Always try to spread the cookies out evenly, so that they bake evenly. Spread them out a little bit smaller than the size of your palm, a standard cookie size will do. Watch the cookies towards the end of bake time or they will burn quickly.

# BIRTHDAY CAKE
*Lemon, strawberry, orange or triple chocolate layer cake*
*Loaded with chocolate chunks*

**Ingredients:**
2 packages (4 squares) IP lemon, strawberry, orange or triple chocolate wafers
2 IP chocolate chip pancake mix (dry)
1 tsp. baking powder
2 large eggs, lightly beaten
½ C. water
Cooking spray
Frosting, for topping, pg. 42

**Directions:**
1. Preheat oven to 350 degrees.
2. Crush wafers by lightly pounding unopened package with a meat mallet, or use a rolling pin to crush.
3. In a medium bowl, mix dry ingredients.

4. Add liquid ingredients; stir to mix.
5. Generously spray two 5" diameter round oven proof bowls; evenly pour ½ the batter into each bowl.
6. Bake 16-18 minutes or until inserted toothpick comes out clean.
7. Cool cakes completely. Frost tops of both cakes and stack.

**Servings:** Entire cake = 4 unrestricted + 4 oz. lean protein; 1/4 cake = 1 unrestricted + 1 oz. lean protein. Count frosting as 'extra' sweetener for the day. Refrigerate or freeze remaining cake quarters for another meal.

# BREAD PUDDING
*With caramel rum sauce*

**Ingredients:** (bread)
1 recipe CinnaVanilla Loaf Bread, pg. 25

**Directions:**
1. Make bread according to directions and cool completely. Once cooled, cut in ½ "cubes; set aside.

**Ingredients:** (egg custard)
**1 T. olive oil, butter flavored (or plain)**
**4 oz. IP premade vanilla drink**
**3 T. liquid egg whites**
**½ tsp. vanilla extract**
**Cooking spray**

**Directions:**
1. Preheat oven to 350 degrees.
2. Place all egg custard ingredients in a large bowl; whisk until oil is well blended. Fold bread cubes into the mixture; let sit 10 – 12 minutes, stirring every 2-3 minutes until bread absorbs egg custard.
3. Spray a 5 3/8" x 3" x 2 1/8" mini loaf pan; add soaked bread mixture. Pat down firmly and evenly.
4. Bake 35 – 40 minutes. Serve with warmed caramel rum sauce.

**Ingredients:** (caramel rum sauce)
**3 T. Walden Farms caramel syrup**
**1-2 drops rum extract**

**Directions:**
1. Place syrup and rum flavoring in a small bowl, heat on high in the microwave 20-30 seconds. Drizzle over bread pudding.

**Servings:** Full loaf = 2 unrestricted; ½ loaf = 1 unrestricted. NOTE: Be sure to count extras in this recipe such as sugar subs. Reserve this recipe fo special occasions.

**TIP:** Store leftover bread pudding in the refrigerator, or wrap tightly and freeze; may eat warm or cold. As an alternative topping for the caramel rum sauce, bread pudding may be served with Strawberry Rhubarb Compote (pg. 45), or Caramel Fried Apples (pg. 38).

## CAPPUCCINO CRISPIES

**Ingredients:**
**1 IP cappuccino drink mix (dry)**
**1 tsp. baking powder**

**1 tsp. sugar free sweetener, granular**
**3 T. liquid egg whites**
**2 tsp. olive oil or grapeseed oil**
**Cooking spray**

**Directions:**
1. Preheat oven to 350 degrees.
2. In a medium bowl, mix together the dry ingredients.
3. Add the liquid ingredients; stir to mix.
4. Drop 6 spoonfuls far apart onto a parchment lined baking sheet.
5. Spray the back of a spoon with cooking spray and spread each cookie to the thickness of a thin mint.
6. Bake 10 - 12 minutes. Cool on cooling rack.

**Servings:** 6 cookies = 1 unrestricted

**TIP:** When spreading the cookies with the back of the spoon, wipe clean from any batter and spray again for each cookie. This will make them much easier to spread.

## CARAMEL APPLE PIE

**Ingredients:**
**½ C. Caramel Fried Apples, pg. 38**
**1 Cinnamon Maple Oatmeal Cookies recipe, raw dough, pg. 40**
**Cooking spray**

**Directions:**
1. Preheat oven to 350 degrees.
2. Place the caramel fried apples in a sprayed individual size (5" diameter) oven proof bowl. Spread cookie dough evenly over the top of the apple mixture and to the edges of the bowl.
3. Bake 15 - 17 minutes or until

inserted toothpick comes clean.
4. Run a knife around the edge of the baked cookie dough, place a plate upside down on top of the bowl and flip over so the caramel fried apples are on top.

**Servings:** 1 unrestricted + 1 C. veggies (1/2 C. caramel fried apples = 1 C. fresh veggies)

## CARAMEL FRIED APPLES
*Crockpot version*

**Ingredients:**
**8 C. chayote squash, skinned and cored, cut in 1" cubes (about 6 chayote)**
**½ C. Walden Farms apple butter spread**
**½ C. Walden Farms caramel syrup**
**½ C. Walden Farms pancake syrup**
**1/3 C. sugar free sweetener, granular (optional)**
**1 T. + 1 tsp. cinnamon**
**1 T. + 1 tsp. lemon juice**

**Directions:**
1. In a medium bowl whisk all ingredients except chayote squash. Place chayote in crockpot; pour caramel mixture over the top. Stir to mix.
2. Cook on high 6 hours.

**Servings:** 8 C. veggies

**TIP:** After cooking, divide into 8 equal portions to get the accurate equivalent to 1 C. servings (raw) as chayote will reduce to about ½ it's volume after cooking. Juice from cooking may be discarded.

## CARAMEL VANILLA LATTE CAKE

**Ingredients:**
1 IP vanilla pudding mix (dry)
1 IP plain pancake mix (dry)
2 tsp. baking powder
1 tsp. sugar free sweetener, granular
1/3 C. liquid egg whites
2 T. cold coffee
2 tsp. olive oil
2 T. Walden Farms caramel syrup
½ tsp. vanilla extract
1 IP caramel and vanilla protein bar
Cooking spray

**Directions:**
1. Preheat oven to 350 degrees.
2. In a medium mixing bowl, combine the dry ingredients except the caramel and vanilla bar; stir to mix.
3. Add the liquid ingredients; stir to mix.
4. Cut the caramel and vanilla bar into 16 pieces. I cut down the middle of the bar lengthwise and then across 8 times to get the 16 pieces. Fold the bar pieces into the batter.
5. Generously spray an oven-proof 5" (1 quart size) round glass bowl with cooking spray.
6. Place batter into the bowl, spray the back of a spoon with cooking spray and lightly spread batter evenly in the bowl.
7. Bake 17 - 19 minutes or until inserted toothpick comes out clean. Cool slightly and cut in wedges.

**Servings:** Entire recipe = 2 unrestricted + 1 restricted

**TIP:** I cut into thirds and eat 1/3 for 1 restricted for the day; save remaining 2 pieces for another serving on another day. Or, I eat 1/3 for breakfast, 1/3 for lunch (with salad and veggies), 1/3 for snack or dessert. All required IP packets for the day are included in this recipe.

## CARROT CAKE

**Ingredients:** (cake)
1 IP vanilla pudding mix (dry)
1 IP maple oatmeal mix (dry)
2 tsp. baking powder
1 tsp. sugar free sweetener, granular
¼ tsp. cinnamon
1/8 tsp. nutmeg
1/8 tsp. ground ginger
1/3 C. liquid egg whites
1 T. milk
2 tsp. olive oil
2 T. Walden Farms caramel syrup
½ tsp. vanilla extract
Cooking spray

**Ingredients:** ('carrots')
½ C. cubed rutabaga
¼ tsp. cinnamon
½ tsp. sugar free sweetener, granular
Olive oil cooking spray

**Directions:**
1. Preheat oven to 425 degrees.
2. Place rutabaga in a medium size bowl. Spray with olive oil cooking spray and sprinkle with cinnamon and sweetener; toss to coat.
3. Place rutabaga cubes far apart on a baking sheet; roast 15-20 minutes or until golden brown, flip once during roasting. Set aside to cool.
4. Turn oven down to 350 degrees.
5. For the cake batter: In a medium mixing bowl, combine the remaining dry ingredients; mix well. Add the liquid ingredients (except rutabaga); stir to mix.
6. Place cooled rutabaga in a food processor and puree. The rutabaga will be grainy, not smooth like puree. Fold pureed rutabaga mixture into the batter.
7. Generously spray an oven-proof 5" (1 quart size) round glass bowl

with cooking spray.
8. Place batter into the bowl, spray the back of a spoon with cooking spray and lightly spread batter evenly in bowl.
9. Bake 22 - 25 minutes or until inserted toothpick comes out clean. Cool. Frost with Frosting if desired, pg. 42.

**Servings:** Entire cake = 2 unrestricted + ½ C. veggies; ½ cake = 1 unrestricted + ¼ C. veggies.

## CHOCOLATE FUDGE BROWNIES

**Ingredients:**
1 IP chocolatey caramel mug cake mix (dry)
1 tsp. cinnamon or pumpkin spice
1 tsp. olive oil
1 T. milk
2 T. Walden Farms chocolate syrup
2 T. liquid egg whites
1 tsp. *Fudge Brownie Flavor Fountain
Cooking spray

**Directions:**
1. Preheat oven to 350 degrees.
2. In a medium bowl, mix the dry ingredients.
3. Add the liquid ingredients; stir to mix.
4. Place batter in a sprayed 12 cavity brownie pan making 2 brownies.
6. Bake 12 minutes.

**Servings:** Entire recipe = 1 unrestricted

**TIP:** *You may purchase the Fudge Brownie Flavor Fountain at www.olivenation.com; this will make the brownies moist and fudge-y in texture, color, and flavor.
Optional: Top with Frosting (basic recipe), pg. 42. As pictured, I added

a few drops orange extract and one drop yellow + one drop red food coloring to the frosting for a pumpkin color.

## CHOCOLATE RHUBARB UPSIDE DOWN CAKE

Ingredients:
2/3 C. Strawberry Rhubarb Compote, pg. 45
1 IP dark chocolate pudding mix (dry)
1 IP chocolate chip pancake mix (dry)
1 tsp. baking powder
1/3 C. liquid egg whites
2 tsp. olive oil
2 T. water
2 T. Walden Farms chocolate syrup
Cooking spray

Directions:
1. Preheat oven to 350 degrees.
2. In a medium bowl, mix together the dry ingredients.
3. Add liquid ingredients (except compote); stir to mix.
4. Spray a 5" round baking pan with cooking spray; evenly spoon the compote into the baking pan. Pour cake batter on top of the compote and level with the back of a sprayed spoon.
5. Bake 18 - 20 minutes or until inserted toothpick comes out clean from center of chocolate batter.
6. Let cool 10 minutes. Run a knife around the edge of the cake to loosen from the baking dish; place a plate face down on top of the dish. Turn the plate and baking dish upside down; serve.

Servings: Entire cake =
2 unrestricted + 1 C. veggies; ½ cake = 1 unrestricted + ½ C. veggies
(2/3 C. compote = 1 C. raw veggies)

TIP: Store any leftover cake in the refrigerator.

## CHOCOLATEY COCONUT ALMOND BROWNIES

Ingredients:
1 IP milk chocolate pudding mix (dry)
1 IP crispy cereal mix (dry), crushed
2 tsp. baking powder
1 tsp. sugar free sweetener, granular
1/3 C. liquid egg whites
1 T. milk
2 tsp. olive oil
2 T. Walden Farms chocolate syrup
1 tsp. coconut extract
½ tsp. almond extract
1 IP chocolatey coconut bar
Cooking spray

Directions:
1. Preheat oven to 350 degrees.
2. In a medium bowl, combine the dry ingredients (except chocolatey coconut bar); stir to mix.
3. Add the liquid ingredients; stir to mix.
4. Cut the chocolatey coconut bar into 16 pieces. I cut down the middle of the bar lengthwise and then across 8 times to get the 16 pieces; fold the bar pieces into the batter.
5. Generously spray an oven-proof 5" (1 quart size) round glass bowl with cooking spray.
6. Place batter into the bowl; lightly spread batter evenly with the back of a sprayed spoon.
7. Bake 17 - 19 minutes or until inserted toothpick comes out clean.

Servings: Entire recipe =
2 unrestricted + 1 restricted

TIP: I cut into thirds and eat 1/3 for 1 restricted for the day; save remaining 2 pieces for another serving on another day. Or, I eat 1/3 for breakfast, 1/3 for lunch (with salad and veggies), 1/3 for snack or dessert. All required IP packets for the day are included in this recipe.

## CINNAMON MAPLE OAT CRUMBLE

Ingredients:
1 IP maple oatmeal mix (dry)
1 ½ tsp. sugar free sweetener, granular
¼ tsp. cinnamon
1 T. water

Directions:
1. Preheat oven to 350 degrees.
2. In a small bowl, mix together dry ingredients.
3. Add water and mix with a fork, pressing the dry mix into the water until ingredients are moist.
4. Place crumble mixture onto a baking sheet and spread out with fingers as much as possible.
5. Bake 5 minutes; remove from oven and crumble with fingers.
6. Bake 1 minute more; remove from oven and crumble again. Let cool.

Servings: 1 unrestricted

TIP: Use this to top Caramel Fried Apples (pg. 38), or Strawberry Rhubarb Compote (pg. 45).

## CINNAMON MAPLE OATMEAL COOKIES

Ingredients:
1 IP maple oatmeal mix (dry)
1 tsp. baking powder
1 tsp. sugar free sweetener, granular
1/8 tsp. cinnamon
3 T. liquid egg whites
2 tsp. olive oil or grapeseed oil
¼ tsp. vanilla extract
1 T. water
Cooking spray

Directions:
1. Preheat oven to 350 degrees.
2. In a medium bowl, mix together the dry ingredients.
3. Add liquid ingredients; stir to mix.
4. Drop 6 spoonfuls batter far apart onto a parchment lined baking sheet.
5. With the back of a sprayed spoon,

spread each cookie to the thickness of a thin mint.
6. Bake 12 minutes. Cool on cooling rack.

**Servings:** 6 cookies = 1 unrestricted

**TIP:** When spreading the cookies with the back of the sprayed spoon, wipe clean from any batter and spray again for each cookie. This will make them much easier to spread.

## COCONUT JOY CUPCAKES
*With chocolate chips*

**Ingredients:**
1 IP vanilla pudding mix, dry
1 IP chocolate chip pancake mix, dry
1 tsp. baking powder
1/3 C. liquid egg whites
2 tsp. olive oil
½ tsp. coconut extract
4 T. water
½ C. shredded zucchini
Cooking spray
Frosting, pg. 42 (optional for topping)

**Directions:**
1. Preheat oven to 350 degrees.
2. In a small bowl, microwave zucchini on high one minute; blot with paper towels to absorb excess moisture. Set aside.
3. In a medium bowl, mix together the dry ingredients.
4. Add liquid ingredients; stir to mix. Fold zucchini into batter.
5. Spray a regular size cupcake tin with cooking spray; spoon batter into cupcake tin making 6 cupcakes.
6. Bake 10 – 12 minutes or until inserted toothpick comes out clean.
7. Cool and frost with chocolate frosting, if desired.

**Servings:** 6 cupcakes = 2 unrestricted; 3 cupcakes = 1 unrestricted

**TIP:** As an alternative to the frosting, drizzle with Walden Farms chocolate syrup.

## COFFEE ICE CREAM

**Ingredients:**
1 IP cappuccino pre-made drink
1 IP cappuccino drink mix (dry)
¼ tsp. vanilla or coffee extract
4 oz. ice water, divided

**Directions:**
1. Put the pre-made cappuccino drink, cappuccino drink mix and extract in a blender; blend well. (Do not add any water at this point.)
2. Evenly divide the cappuccino mixture in half by pouring into two separate plastic containers with lids.
3. Freeze solid; this will take a few hours.
4. For one serving, remove one of the containers from the freezer and place in a warm water bath to loosen the frozen ice cream from the container.
5. When the ice cream has melted a bit, place it back in the blender and add 2 oz. ice water; blend well and serve. (The remaining 2 oz. of cold water will be used for the second serving of ice cream.)

**Servings:** Entire recipe = 2 unrestricted; ½ recipe = 1 unrestricted

## DOUBLE CHOCOLATE CHIP COOKIES
*Soft and cake-like*

**Ingredients:**
1 IP chocolatey caramel mug cake mix (dry)
1 tsp. olive oil
1 T. milk
2 T. Walden Farms chocolate syrup
2 T. liquid egg whites
½ tsp. *fudge brownie flavor fountain (optional)
Cooking spray

**Directions:**
1. Preheat oven to 350 degrees.
2. In a medium bowl, mix all ingredients.
3. Place batter in a sprayed muffin top pan making 2 cookies; spread evenly. (If you don't have a muffin top pan, divide the batter in half and spread two 3 inch circles on a parchment lined baking sheet).
4. Bake 7-9 minutes or until centers are done. Do not over bake or they will become very dry.
5. Let cool a few minutes; place in the toaster and lightly toast. This will give the outside of the cookie a crispier outside texture.

**Servings:** 1 unrestricted

**TIP:** *The fudge brownie flavor fountain may be purchased at www.olivenation.com. It is not necessary for this recipe; however, it will add a rich fudge color and flavor.

## EGGNOG CRISPIES

**Ingredients:**
1 IP vanilla drink mix (dry)
1 tsp. baking powder
1 tsp. sugar free sweetener, granular
1/8 tsp. nutmeg
3 T. liquid egg whites
2 tsp. olive oil or grapeseed oil
1/8 tsp. rum extract, sugar free
Cooking spray

**Directions:**
1. Preheat oven to 350 degrees.
2. In a medium bowl, mix together the dry ingredients.
3. Add the liquid ingredients; stir to mix.
4. Drop 6 spoonfuls far apart onto a parchment lined baking sheet.
5. Spray the back of a spoon with cooking spray and spread each cookie to the thickness of a thin mint. Spray the spoon before spreading each cookie or batter will stick to the spoon.
6. Bake 10 - 12 minutes. Cool on cooling rack.

**Servings:** 6 cookies = 1 unrestricted

## FROSTING
*Basic Recipe*

**Ingredients:**
2 T. IP pudding mix (dry), any flavor
2 T. liquid egg whites
1 T. cold water
¼ - ½ tsp. extract or emulsion (sugar free), any flavor
¼ tsp. cinnamon (optional)

**Directions:**
1. In a small bowl, combine all ingredients.
2. Using an electric hand beater, beat to a smooth frosting consistency. The longer the frosting is beaten, the stiffer it will become.
3. Refrigerate in an airtight container until use.

**Servings:** This will frost 6 cupcakes. I count this as sugar sub extras for the day.

**TIP:** A wide variety of flavors may be made using this basic recipe. Do not use real egg whites as they are not always pasteurized; use only liquid egg whites.

## GINGERBREAD COOKIES

**Ingredients:**
1 IP apple cinnamon soy puffs
1/8 tsp. baking powder
1 tsp. sugar free sweetener, granular
Pinch of ground cloves
Pinch of ground ginger
Pinch of nutmeg
3 T. water
Cooking spray

**Directions:**
1. Preheat oven to 350 degrees.
2. Add dry ingredients to a blender or food processor; blend to fine crumbs.
3. Transfer to a small bowl; add water and mix.
4. Evenly drop 6 spoonfuls of batter onto a parchment lined baking sheet.
5. Spread into thin circles with the back of a spoon sprayed with cooking spray; you may also pat down with your fingers.

6. Bake 10 minutes; take out of oven and flip. Bake another 5 minutes.

**Servings:** 6 cookies = 1 restricted

**TIP:** Always try to spread the cookies out evenly, so that they bake evenly. Spread them out a little bit smaller than the size of your palm; a standard cookie size will do. Watch the cookies towards the end of bake time or they will burn quickly.

## GLAZE
*Great for topping quick breads, donuts, cupcakes and more!*

**Ingredients:**
2 T. Walden Farms marshmallow dip
2 tsp. Walden Farms pancake syrup
½ tsp. cinnamon, optional
¼ tsp. extract (any flavor), optional

**Directions:**
1. Add all ingredients to a small bowl and whisk with a fork until mixed.
2. Drizzle over finished baked goods.

**Servings:** Use 1 T. per serving and count as a sugar free substitute extra; cover and refrigerate remainder of unused glaze for another time.

## GRANOLA COOKIES

**Ingredients:**
1 IP vanilla crispy square, cut in 4-6 pieces
1 IP packet sweet & spicy trail mix
1 T. liquid egg whites
Cooking spray

**Directions:**
1. Preheat oven to 300 degrees.
2. Place all ingredients in a food processor; process until crispy square has completely blended to crumbs and mixed well with the trail mix.

NOTE: Some of the trail mix nuts will not completely break down; this is what you want.
3. Spray a regular size muffin tin with cooking spray. Fill muffin tin with mixture, making 8 cookies; pat down cookies by pressing firmly with the flats of your fingernails as they won't stick to the mixture.
4. Bake 4-5 minutes or until edges just start to lightly brown.
5. Remove from oven and cool in the muffin pan on cooling rack at least 5+ minutes. (If you omit this step, they will not stick together as well.)
6. Carefully remove from pan and continue to cool at least 5 more minutes.

**Servings:** 8 cookies = 2 unrestricted; 4 cookies = 1 unrestricted

## HUNKY MONKEY CUPCAKES
*A favorite recipe for chocolate and banana lovers*

**Ingredients:**
1 IP vanilla pudding mix (dry)
1 IP chocolate chip pancake mix (dry)
1 tsp. baking powder
1 tsp. sugar free sweetener, granular
1/3 C. liquid egg whites
2 tsp. olive oil
¼ tsp. banana extract
2 T. Walden Farms chocolate syrup
2 T. water
Cooking spray
Frosting, pg. 42

**Directions:**
1. Preheat oven to 350 degrees.
2. In a medium bowl, mix together the dry ingredients.
3. Add liquid ingredients; stir to mix.
4. Spray a regular size cupcake tin with cooking spray; spoon batter into cupcake tin making 6 cupcakes.
5. Bake 10 - 12 minutes.
6. Cool completely; frost.

Servings: 6 cupcakes =
2 unrestricted; 3 cupcakes =
1 unrestricted

## ICE CREAM SMOOTHIE

*A 900+ watt blender is
recommended for this recipe*

Ingredients:
1 IP pudding mix (dry), any flavor
1 C. ice cold water
2 C. ice, divided
1 tsp. vanilla extract (or other flavor)

Directions:
1. Place the dry pudding mix, ice cold water and extract in the large blender container; blend.
2. Add 1 cup ice; blend well.
3. Add the remaining 1 cup ice and blend to ice cream consistency. Container may need to be opened during blending process to move the mixture around with a spoon making sure it is well blended.
4. Serve immediately. This ice cream cannot be refrozen.

Servings: 1 IP unrestricted

## MARDI GRAS KING CAKE

Ingredients: (cake)
1 IP vanilla pudding mix (dry)
1 IP plain pancake mix (dry)
1 tsp. baking powder
1 tsp. sugar free sweetener, granular (optional)
1/3 C. liquid egg whites
2 tsp. olive oil
1 tsp. *cream cheese emulsion (or ½ tsp. vanilla extract)
3 T. + 2 tsp. water
Cooking spray

Ingredients: (filling)
Cinnamon, to taste
3 tsp. Walden Farms raspberry spread

Directions: (cake + filling)
1. Preheat oven to 350 degrees.
2. In a medium bowl, mix together the dry ingredients for the CAKE.
3. Add the CAKE liquid ingredients; stir to mix.

4. Spray a 5 3/8" x 3" x 2 1/8" mini loaf pan with cooking spray; pour ½ the batter into pan and smooth with the back of a sprayed spoon.
5. For the FILLING: Sprinkle the top of the batter with a dusting of cinnamon; place the raspberry spread, 1 tsp. at a time, across the middle of the cake.
6. Pour the remaining cake batter on top and smooth with the back of a sprayed spoon.
7. Bake 19 - 21 minutes or until an inserted toothpick comes out clean.
8. Cool completely and glaze (recipe to follow). It is important to cool completely or the texture will be spongy; once cooled, it is delicious.

Ingredients: (cream cheese glaze)
2 T. Walden Farms marshmallow dip
1 tsp. Walden Farms pancake syrup
1 tsp. *cream cheese emulsion (or ½ tsp. vanilla extract)

Directions:
1. Place ingredients in a small bowl and vigorously whisk with a fork or whisk until blended; frost cooled King Cake.

Ingredients: (colored icing drizzle)
3 T. Walden Farms marshmallow dip
3 tsp. Walden Farm pancake syrup
¾ tsp. vanilla extract
2 drops yellow food coloring
2 drops green food coloring
2 drops blue + 3 drops red food coloring (for purple color)

Directions:
1. Divide the 3 T. Walden Farms marshmallow dip by placing 1 T. into 3 small separate bowls.
2. Add ¼ tsp. vanilla extract to each bowl.
3. Add 2 drops yellow food coloring to the first bowl, 2 drops green food coloring to the second bowl and 2

drops blue + 3 drops red food coloring to the third bowl. Stir ingredients in each bowl till mixed, using a separate fork for each so the colors don't mix.
4. Using 3 separate baggies, place one color into one corner of each of the bags. Snip a tiny bit of a corner off each bag; drizzle colored icings over the top of the cake.

Servings: Entire cake = 2 unrestricted; ½ cake = 1 unrestricted. NOTE: Be sure to count extras in this recipe such as sugar subs, Walden Farms, etc. Reserve this recipe for special occasions.

TIP: *You may purchase the cream cheese emulsion at www.olivenation.com.

## MOCHA FROZEN CUSTARD ICE CREAM

*A 900+ watt blender is
recommended for this recipe*

Ingredients:
1 IP cappuccino pre-made drink
1 IP dark or milk chocolate pudding mix (dry)
¼ tsp. coffee extract, sugar free (optional)
4 oz. ice cold water, divided

Directions:
1. Put the pre-made cappuccino drink, pudding mix and extract in a blender; blend well. Do not add any water at this point.
2. Evenly divide the mocha mix in half by pouring into two separate plastic containers with lids.
3. Freeze solid; this will take a few hours.
4. For one serving, remove one container from freezer and place in a

warm water bath to loosen the frozen ice cream from the container.
5.  When the ice cream has melted a bit, place it back in the blender and add 2 oz. of ice cold water; blend well and serve.  The remaining 2 oz. of cold water will be used for the second serving of ice cream.

**Servings:** Entire recipe = 2 unrestricted; ½ recipe = 1 unrestricted

## ORANGE CREAMSICLE CUPCAKES

**Ingredients:**
1 IP vanilla pudding mix (dry)
1 IP plain pancake mix (dry)
2 tsp. baking powder
1/3 C. liquid egg whites
1 T. milk
1 tsp. olive oil
1 T. Walden Farms orange marmalade
1 tsp. cream cheese emulsion
 (or ½ tsp. vanilla extract)
¼ tsp. orange extract
2 T. water
Cooking spray
Frosting, pg. 42

**Directions:**
1.  Preheat oven to 350 degrees.
2.  In a medium bowl, mix together the dry ingredients.
3.  Place the orange marmalade in a small bowl and heat on high in the microwave for 15 seconds; stir.
4.  Add liquid ingredients, including marmalade.  Stir to mix.
5.  Coat a regular size muffin/cupcake tin with cooking spray; spoon batter into muffin/cupcake tin making 6 cupcakes.
6.  Bake 12 - 14 minutes.  Cool and frost, if desired.

**Servings:** 6 cupcakes = 2 unrestricted; 3 cupcakes = 1 unrestricted

**TIP:** You may purchase the cream cheese emulsion from www.olivenation.com.

## PEANUT BUTTER COOKIES
*Crispy and delicious*

**Ingredients:**
1 pkg. IP peanut butter soy puffs
1/8 tsp. baking powder
1 tsp. sugar free sweetener, granular
2 T. + 1 ½ tsp. water
Cooking spray

**Directions:**
1. Preheat oven to 350 degrees.
2. Add dry ingredients to a blender or food processor; blend to fine crumbs.
3. Transfer to a small bowl; add water and mix.
4. Evenly drop 6 spoonfuls of batter onto a parchment lined baking sheet.
5. Spread into thin circles with the back of a spoon sprayed with cooking spray; you may also pat down with your fingers.
6. Bake 10 minutes; take out of oven and flip.  Bake another 5 minutes.

**Servings:** 6 cookies = 1 restricted

**TIP:** Always try to spread the cookies out evenly so that they bake evenly. Spread them out a little bit smaller than the size of your palm; a standard cookie size will do.  Watch the cookies towards the end of bake time or they will burn quickly.

## PUMPKIN PIE COOKIES

**Ingredients:**
1 pkg. IP peanut butter soy puffs
1/8 tsp. baking powder
1 tsp. sugar free sweetener, granular
¼ tsp. pumpkin pie spice
2 T. + 1 ½ tsp. water
Cooking spray

**Directions:**
1. Preheat oven to 350 degrees.
2. Add dry ingredients to a blender or food processor; blend to fine crumbs.
3. Transfer to a small bowl; add water and mix.
4. Evenly drop 6 spoonfuls of batter onto a parchment lined baking sheet.
5. Spread into thin circles with the back of a spoon sprayed with cooking

spray; you may also pat down with your fingers.
6. Bake 10 minutes; take out of oven and flip.  Bake another 5 minutes.

**Servings:**  6 cookies = 1 restricted

**TIP:**  Always try to spread the cookies out evenly so that they bake evenly. Spread them out a little bit smaller than the size of your palm; a standard cookie size will do.  Watch the cookies towards the end of bake time or they will burn quickly.

## RED VELVET CUPCAKES
*This is a no fail cupcake recipe for Red Velvet chocolate lovers*

**Ingredients:**
1 IP milk or dark chocolate pudding mix (dry)
1 IP plain or chocolate chip pancake mix (dry)
1 tsp. baking powder
1 tsp. sugar free sweetener, granular
1/3 C. liquid egg whites
1 tsp. olive oil
3 T. + 1 tsp. water
1 tsp. *red velvet emulsion
Cooking spray

**Directions:**
1.  Preheat oven to 350 degrees.
2.  In a medium bowl, mix together dry ingredients.
3.  Add liquid ingredients; stir to mix.
4.  Spray a regular size muffin/ cupcake tin; evenly divide batter making 6 cupcakes.
5.  Bake 11 - 13 minutes or until inserted toothpick comes out clean.
6.  Cool completely.  Drizzle with Glaze (pg. 42), if desired.

**Servings:** 6 cupcakes = 2  unrestricted;  3 cupcakes = 1 unrestricted

TIP: *You may purchase the red velvet emulsion at www.olivenation.com.

# RHUBARB DUMP CAKE

**Ingredients:**
2/3 C. Strawberry Rhubarb
Compote, pg. 45
1 IP vanilla pudding mix (dry)
1 IP pancake mix, any flavor
1 tsp. baking powder
1 tsp. sugar free sweetener, granular
½ tsp. cinnamon
1/3 C. liquid egg whites
4 T. water
2 tsp. olive oil
1 tsp. vanilla extract
Cooking spray

**Directions:**
1. Preheat oven to 350 degrees.
2. In a medium mixing bowl, add dry ingredients; stir to mix.
3. Add the liquid ingredients (except compote); stir to mix.
4. Generously spray an oven-proof 5 inch (1 quart) round baking dish.
5. Evenly spread Strawberry Rhubarb Compote in glass bowl. Scoop cake batter over the top of compote and evenly spread batter to the sides of the bowl with the back of a sprayed spoon.
6. Bake for 22 - 25 minutes or until an inserted toothpick comes out clean.
7. Refrigerate any leftovers.

**Servings:** Entire cake = 2 unrestricted + 1 C. veggies (2/3 C. compote = 1 C. raw veggies); ½ cake = 1 unrestricted + ½ C. veggies

**TIP:** A mini loaf pan may be used as an alternative to the 5 inch round baking dish. I use a 5 3/8" x 3" x 2 1/8" mini loaf pan. This cake is delicious served hot or cold; a perfect snack or lunch idea.

# SNICKERDOODLE COOKIES

**Ingredients:**
1 IP vanilla drink mix (dry)
1 tsp. baking powder
1 tsp. sugar free sweetener, granular
½ tsp. cinnamon
3 T. liquid egg whites
2 tsp. olive oil or grapeseed oil
¼ tsp. butter extract (or vanilla extract)
Cooking spray

**Directions:**
1. Preheat oven to 350 degrees.
2. In a medium bowl, mix together dry ingredients.
3. Add liquid ingredients; stir to mix.
4. Drop 6 spoonfuls batter far apart onto a parchment lined baking sheet.
5. With the back of a sprayed spoon, spread each cookie to the thickness of a thin mint. Spray the spoon before flattening each cookie or batter will stick.
6. Bake 10 - 12 minutes.

**Servings:** 6 cookies = 1 unrestricted

# STRAWBERRY RHUBARB COBBLER

**Ingredients:**
2/3 C. Strawberry Rhubarb
Compote, pg. 45
1 Cinnamon Maple Oatmeal Cookies recipe, (raw dough) pg. 40

**Directions:**
1. Preheat oven to 350 degrees.
2. Place the compote in an individual size oven proof bowl.
3. Spread cookie dough over the top of the compote.
4. Bake 15 - 17 minutes.

**Servings:** 1 unrestricted + 1 C. veggies (1 C. rhubarb = 2/3 C. rhubarb compote)

# STRAWBERRY RHUBARB COMPOTE

**Ingredients:**
3 C. fresh or frozen rhubarb, (cut into 1" chunks)
2 T. Walden Farms strawberry syrup
1 T. Walden Farms pancake syrup
1 tsp. lemon juice
¼ tsp. cinnamon
½ tsp. vanilla extract

**Directions:**
1. Place all ingredients in a medium sauce pan; stir to mix. Bring to a boil over medium high heat.
2. Turn down heat to medium low; simmer 10 minutes, stirring occasionally, or cook until rhubarb is stewed to desired consistency.
3. Divide rhubarb mixture into 3 equal portions. Refrigerate till cool or cold.

**Servings:** Entire recipe = 3 C. veggies; 1/3 recipe = 1 C. veggies

**TIP:** 1 C. raw rhubarb = 2/3 C. rhubarb compote (cooked)

# STRAWBERRY RHUBARB PUDDING PARFAIT

**Ingredients:**
2/3 C. Strawberry Rhubarb
Compote, pg. 45
1 IP pudding mix, prepared (any flavor)

**Directions:**
1. Prepare pudding mix according to package directions.
2. In a parfait glass, layer the rhubarb mixture and then the pudding; repeat, making several layers. End with pudding on top.
3. Chill in the refrigerator 1 - 2 hours. Serve cold.

**Servings:** 1 unrestricted + 1 C. veggies (1 C. rhubarb = 2/3 C. rhubarb compote, cooked)

## TIE DYE CAKE
*Create holiday color themes or use colors of your favorite sports team*

**Ingredients:**
1 IP vanilla pudding mix (dry)
1 IP plain pancake mix (dry)
1 tsp. baking powder
1 tsp. sugar free sweetener, granular (optional)
1/3 C. liquid egg whites
2 tsp. olive oil
4 T. water
Food coloring, any colors of choice
Glaze, pg. 42 (for topping)
Cooking spray

**Directions:**
1. Preheat oven to 350 degrees.
2. In a medium bowl, mix together the dry ingredients.
3. Add liquid ingredients except food

coloring; stir to mix.
4. Divide the batter evenly into 3 separate bowls. Add your choice of food coloring (desired amount for color) to one bowl; mix. Add another choice of food coloring (desired amount for color) to second bowl; mix. You will leave the remaining batter in the third bowl as white (no food coloring.)
5. Spray a 5" round cake pan with cooking spray; spoon batter randomly from each colored batter into the pan making a multicolored batter. Using a fork, make a circular swirl to make the tie dye effect.
6. Bake 18 – 22 minutes or until an inserted toothpick comes out clean.
7. Cool and drizzle with glaze, if desired.

**Servings:** Entire cake = 2 unrestricted; ½ cake = 1 unrestricted

## WHOOPIE PIES
*Stuffed with marshmallow crème*

**Ingredients:** (whoopie pie)
1 IP dark or milk chocolate pudding mix, (dry)
1 IP chocolate chip or plain pancake mix (dry)
1 tsp. baking powder
1/3 C. liquid egg whites
2 tsp. olive oil
4 T. water
Cooking spray

**Ingredients:** (filling)
2-3 T. Walden Farms marshmallow dip
½ tsp. vanilla extract

**Directions:**
1. Preheat oven to 350 degrees.
2. In a medium bowl, mix dry ingredients.
3. Add liquid ingredients. Stir to mix.

4. Spray a whoopie pie pan or muffin top tin with cooking spray; spoon batter into tin making 4 pies.
5. Bake 8 minutes; cool.
6. In a small bowl, whisk together the filling ingredients until smooth and creamy.
7. Spread ½ the mixture on 1 muffin top and top with the second muffin top to make a whoopie pie. Reserve the remaining filling and refrigerate until ready to serve and eat the second whoopie pie.

**Servings:** 2 whoopie pies = 2 unrestricted; 1 whoopie pie = 1 unrestricted

**TIP:** Eat at room temperature or freeze for an ice cream-like sandwich. If you don't have a muffin top or whoopie pie pan, line a baking sheet with parchment paper (not wax paper) and form four 3" circles; bake as directed.

## ZUCCHINI FRIED APPLES

**Ingredients:**
3 C. *sliced zucchini (peel off)
2 tsp. olive oil
1 tsp. lemon juice
½ - 1 tsp. cinnamon
1 T. Walden Farms caramel syrup
1 T. Walden Farms pancake syrup
1 T. Walden Farms apple butter (if you don't have this, use extra syrup)

**Directions:**
1. Heat olive oil in a frying pan over medium/medium hi heat. Add lemon juice and zucchini; stir fry until golden brown.
2. Add remaining ingredients; cook 3-5 minutes while gently stirring.
3. Place in a covered container and refrigerate until ready to use.

**Servings:** 3 C. veggies

**TIP:** *When prepping zucchini for this dish, cut zucchini lengthwise in half. Run a spoon down the center of each half to scoop out any soft seed/flesh area. Cut ½" slices crosswise; they will look like apple slices.

# Dressings, Sauces, Seasonings & Condiments

**TIP:** There are essentially 2 ways to amp up flavor to a dish - fat or seasonings, herbs and spices. Since we are limited with fats, experiment with the latter. It's a great way to introduce flavor to a dish without adding extra calories. From there, the cooking technique will help to amp the flavor of most any dish.

**Rhubarb BBQ Sauce**
**Page 50**

**Lebanese Garlic Lemon Dressing**
**Page 49**

**Thai Dressing**
**Page 52**

**Rich and Sassy BBQ Sauce**
**Page 51**

**Mockamole**
**Page 50**

**Spaghizza Sauce**
**Page 51**

## APPLE RHUBARB CHUTNEY
*Excellent served over pork chops or pork tenderloin*

Ingredients:
3 C. sliced rhubarb
2 C. cubed chayote squash
1 T. apple cider vinegar
¼ C. Walden Farms pancake syrup
¼ tsp. orange extract
¼ tsp. ground cloves
¼ tsp. cinnamon
¼ tsp. nutmeg
¼ tsp. ground ginger
1/8 tsp. salt
1/8 tsp. pepper

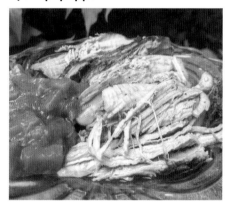

Directions:
1. Place chayote in a microwave proof bowl; cover and cook on high 8 minutes. Drain.
2. In a medium sauce pan, add all ingredients including chayote. Bring to a boil over medium high heat, stirring constantly.
3. Turn down heat to medium-low; simmer 1 hour stirring every 15 minutes.

Servings: Entire recipe = 5 C. veggies; 1/5 recipe = 1 C. veggies

TIP: After cooking down chutney, divide equally into 5 portions. Each portion will be equivalent to 1 C. veggies.

## BEST GRAVY EVER

Ingredients:
1 C. cubed chayote squash
1 C. (3.5 oz.) cauliflower florets
1 C. sliced cabbage
2 C. chicken or beef broth (or 1 C. each), fat free
Garlic powder, to taste
Salt and pepper, to taste
Olive oil spray

Directions:
1. Preheat oven to 425 degrees.
2. Cut off the end of the chayote squash, peel off the skin with a potato peeler and cut in half. Remove center membrane and cube. Set aside.
3. Cut cauliflower florets in quarter inch slices.
4. Spray 2 baking sheets with olive oil. Place chayote on one, the sliced cabbage and cauliflower on the other; space them out as much as possible.
5. Lightly spray the veggies with olive oil and sprinkle with garlic powder.
6. Roast the cabbage and cauliflower for about 15 minutes, the chayote for about 20 minutes or until the veggies are lightly browned. Turn once during roasting.
7. Remove veggies from oven when done and place in a high speed 900+ watt blender.
8. Add broth and puree to a smooth consistency.
9. Put gravy in a sauce pan on medium heat and heat through, stirring constantly. Season with salt and pepper.

Servings: Entire recipe = 3 C. veggies

TIP: This is amazing on Cauliflower Mashed Faux-tatoes (pg. 90).

## CAULIFLOWER HUMMUS

Ingredients:
4 C. (14 oz.) cauliflower florets, cut in bite size pieces
4 tsp. extra virgin olive oil
1 tsp. smoked paprika
½ tsp. garlic powder
1 tsp. kosher salt
½ tsp. ground cumin
¼ tsp. red pepper flakes
1 T. lemon juice
1/3 C. chicken broth, fat free

Directions:
1. Preheat oven to 425 degrees. Place cauliflower florets, olive oil and dry seasonings in a resealable bag. Shake to coat florets.
2. Spread florets onto a baking sheet. Roast 20-23 minutes, flipping once during roasting.
3. Place roasted florets and remaining ingredients in a blender or food processor; blend. You may add more chicken broth if necessary for desired texture.

Servings: Entire recipe = 4 C. veggies; ¼ recipe = 1 C. veggies

## CHIMICHURRI SAUCE
*Excellent Argentine condiment for grilled steak, chicken or pork*

Ingredients:
1 C. fresh Italian parsley, trimmed of thick stems and firmly packed
1 C. fresh cilantro, trimmed of thick

stems and firmly packed
3 - 4 garlic cloves
2 T. fresh oregano leaves (may substitute 2 tsp. dried oregano)
½ C. olive oil
2 T. apple cider vinegar or white vinegar
1 tsp. sea salt
¼ tsp. freshly ground black pepper
¼ tsp. crushed red pepper flakes

**Directions:**
1. Place all ingredients in a blender or food processor and pulse just until blended; no need to puree unless that is the preferred consistency.
2. Adjust seasonings as desired.
3. Serve at room temperature; refrigerate leftovers.

**TIP:** Serve as a condiment with lean cooked meats; exceptionally good served with flank steak.

## EXTRA VIRGIN DIJON DRESSING

**Ingredients:**
2 T. water
1 T. apple cider vinegar
1 clove garlic, minced
2 tsp. Dijon mustard
Pinch each salt & pepper
2 T. extra virgin olive oil

**Directions:**
1. In a small bowl, whisk together water, vinegar, garlic, mustard, salt

and pepper.
2. Gradually whisk in olive oil.

## GINGER SOY VINAIGRETTE

**Ingredients:**
2 T. apple cider vinegar
¼ tsp. ground ginger
1/3 C. olive oil
1 T. soy sauce
¼ tsp. sugar free sweetener, granular
¼ tsp. IP salt
¼ tsp. black pepper
¼ tsp. hot pepper sauce (sugar free)

**Directions:**
1. In a medium bowl, mix together the vinegar, ginger, soy sauce, sweetener, salt, pepper and hot pepper sauce.
2. Whisk in oil. Shake or whisk before serving.

## GREEK SEASONING

**Ingredients:**
2 tsp. salt
2 tsp. dried basil
2 tsp. dried oregano
½ tsp. dried thyme
2 tsp. garlic powder
1 tsp. dried dill weed
1 tsp. marjoram
1 tsp. black pepper
1 tsp. parsley flakes
1 tsp. rosemary
½ tsp. cinnamon
½ tsp. nutmeg

**Directions:**
1. Mix well; store in an airtight container.

## LEBANESE GARLIC LEMON DRESSING

**Ingredients:**
½ C. fresh lemon juice
½ C. extra virgin olive oil
3 cloves garlic, minced
1 tsp. kosher or sea salt
1/8 tsp. black pepper

**Directions:**
1. In a medium bowl, whisk together all ingredients.
2. Whisk or shake before serving.

## MANGO SALSA
*Excellent on Blackened Grilled Mahi Mahi, pg. 56*

**Ingredients:**
1/3 C. diced yellow bell peppers
1/3 C. diced tomatoes
¼ C. diced red onion
1 T. chopped fresh cilantro
1 T. IP mango pre-made drink
Salt, to taste

**Directions:**
1. In a small bowl, combine all ingredients.
2. Refrigerate until use.

**Servings:** 1 C. veggies

## MAPLE SOY VINAIGRETTE

Ingredients:
½ C. soy sauce
½ C. cider vinegar
½ C. Walden Farms pancake syrup
2 T. sugar free sweetener, granular
2 T. Dijon mustard
1 small clove garlic, finely chopped
½ tsp. ground ginger
¼ tsp. IP salt
¼ tsp. black pepper
½ C. olive oil

Directions:
1. In a blender, mix all ingredients together except oil.
2. Slowly drizzle oil into the blender; blend until thickened.
3. Adjust seasonings to taste.
4. Serve at room temperature.

## MOCKAMOLE

Ingredients:
1¾ C. asparagus, cut in 1" pieces
1 T. lime juice
3 T. Pico de Gallo Salsa, pg. 50
¼ C. chopped fresh cilantro
¼ C. chopped green onion
½ jalapeno pepper, minced
1 tsp. minced garlic
1 or 2 dashes red hot sauce
Salt and pepper, to taste

Directions:
1. Cut asparagus spears in 1" pieces. Cut off any tough ends and discard.
2. Place asparagus in a steamer on stovetop and steam, covered, for 10 minutes.
3. Put steamed asparagus in a food processor; puree until smooth. Place in a covered container and refrigerate until cool.
4. Place cooled asparagus puree in a medium bowl; fold in remaining ingredients.
5. Store in refrigerator.

Servings: 2 C. veggies

## PICO DE GALLO SALSA

Ingredients:
1½ C. diced fresh Roma tomatoes
1 C. diced yellow or red onion
2/3 C. chopped fresh cilantro
1 - 2 jalapeno peppers, seeded and finely chopped
Juice of ½ lime, or to taste
Sea salt, to taste

Directions:
1. In a medium bowl, gently combine tomatoes, onion, cilantro and jalapeno.
2. Remove any seeds from the lime half; squeeze juice over the Pico de Gallo mixture. Sprinkle with sea salt; gently mix to blend in juice and salt.
3. Taste the Pico de Gallo Salsa; adjust salt, lime, jalapeno or cilantro as desired. Store in a covered container in refrigerator.

Servings: Varies; I measure the Pico de Gallo Salsa as I use it to get the veggie serving count.

## RASPBERRY GARLIC VINAIGRETTE

Ingredients:
1 T. Walden Farms raspberry dressing
½ tsp. garlic and herb seasoning blend
1 T. olive oil

Directions:
1. Stir together all ingredients. Drizzle over salad and toss.

TIP: Use as a dipping sauce for celery or cucumbers.

## RHUBARB BBQ SAUCE

Ingredients:
3 C. sliced rhubarb, 1" chunks
2 ¼ C. tomato sauce
¼ C. + 2 T. dried minced onion
1 ½ tsp. garlic powder
¾ C. apple cider vinegar
1/3 C. + 2 T. Walden Farms or IP pancake syrup
¼ C. + 2 T. tomato paste
1 ½ tsp. smoked paprika
1 tsp. black pepper
1 ½ tsp. smoked salt
1 tsp. chili powder
1 T. sugar free sweetener, granular

Directions:
1. Place all ingredients in a medium sauce pan and bring to a boil; immediately reduce heat and simmer 20 minutes, uncovered, stirring occasionally.

2. Mash rhubarb mixture with a fork for a chunkier sauce, or puree in a blender for a smoother sauce.
3. Taste and adjust seasonings to your liking, if desired.

**Servings:** Entire recipe = 8 C. veggies (rhubarb, tomato sauce, dried onions and tomato paste)

**TIP:** After preparing sauce, divide into 8 equal servings – those servings, no matter their weight or volume, will be equivalent to 1 C. veggies consumed. Dividing into 16 portions will be equivalent to ½ C. veggies consumed, and so on.

# RICH AND SASSY BBQ SAUCE

**Ingredients:**
1 C. Walden Farms ketchup
1 T. olive oil
1 T. onion powder
1 T. lemon juice
1 T. sugar free sweetener, granular
1 tsp. minced garlic
1 tsp. chili powder
1 T. liquid smoke, sugar free
1 T. apple cider vinegar
½ tsp. salt
½ tsp. black pepper

**Directions:**
1. In a small saucepan, combine all ingredients and simmer, covered, for 20 minutes. Remove cover and simmer an additional 5 minutes.
2. Store BBQ sauce in refrigerator; heat before serving.

**Servings:** Use in moderation.

# SAUSAGE SEASONING

**Ingredients:**
3 ½ tsp. paprika
1 ½ tsp. IP salt
½ + ¼ tsp. garlic powder
1 tsp. fennel seed
1 tsp. pepper
¼ tsp. crushed red pepper flakes, optional

**Directions:**
1. In a small bowl, mix all ingredients together.
2. Store mixture in an airtight container until ready for use.

**TIP:** This is a dry herb seasoning that may be added to lean ground pork, beef, chicken or turkey to give the meat a sausage flavor. One recipe of seasoning is enough to season 1 lb. of meat. If a milder flavor is desired, the crushed red pepper flakes may be omitted. The recipe may be doubled or tripled as needed. If a finer consistency is desired, the ingredients may be blended in a spice grinder or mini food processor.

# SOFRITO
*For uses, see TIP following recipe*

**Ingredients:**
2 C. (10.6 oz.) green bell peppers, cut in chunks
1 C. (5.3 oz.) red bell pepper, cut in chunks
2 C. (12.6 oz.) fresh tomato, cut in chunks

1 C. chopped green onion
10 – 12 garlic cloves, peeled
1 C. fresh cilantro, firmly packed
½ C. fresh Italian parsley, firmly packed
1 tsp. kosher salt
½ tsp. black pepper

**Directions:**
1. Place all ingredients in a food processor; blend to the consistency of a pesto.
2. Drain in a mesh strainer; store covered in fridge.

**Servings:** Entire recipe = 6 C. veggies

**TIP:** There are several uses for this Latin inspired condiment to add extra flavor to any dish. Add to soups, stews or egg dishes. Top casseroles, cauliflower rice, cooked lean meats, fish or seafood. Makes a great dip for chips and crackers. Freezes well; divide in portions and wrap or seal well. To Freeze: Place 2 T. in each cavity of an ice cube tray and freeze; once frozen, put cubes in an airtight resealable plastic bag and store in freezer; 2 cubes = ¼ C. veggies.

# SPAGHIZZA SAUCE
*A great sauce for spaghetti, pizza and other dishes requiring an Italian tomato sauce*

**Ingredients:**
28 oz. can crushed tomatoes
2 T. tomato paste
¼ tsp. black pepper
½ tsp. crushed red pepper flakes
1 tsp. onion powder
1 tsp. garlic powder

1 T. Italian seasoning
1 tsp. salt
2 T. apple cider vinegar
2 T. extra virgin olive oil

**Directions:**
1. Place all ingredients in a blender; blend until tomatoes are pureed. Taste; adjust seasonings if necessary.
2. Pour mixture into a medium sauce pan and bring to a low boil. Immediately turn down to low heat; simmer for 25 - 30 minutes, stirring occasionally. Refrigerate sauce until use.

**Servings:** Entire recipe = 5 C. veggies; after cooking, evenly divide sauce into 5 separate servings. Each serving is equivalent to 1 C. veggies no matter the volume.

**TIP:** The longer the sauce is simmered, the thicker it will get. When buying canned tomatoes, check the INGREDIENTS list, not the NUTRITION label for added sugar. There will be some sugar listed in the nutrition label from the natural sugars in the tomatoes.

## SWEET & SOUR SAUCE

**Ingredients:**
½ C. sugar free sweetener, granular
1/3 C. apple cider vinegar
2 T. Walden Farms ketchup
2 T. tomato paste
1 T. Walden Farms or IP pancake syrup
1 T. soy sauce
½ tsp. garlic powder

**Directions:**
1. In a medium mixing bowl, whisk all ingredients together until thoroughly mixed.
2. Refrigerate.

**Servings:** Entire recipe = ¼ C. veggies (tomato paste); ½ recipe = 2 T. veggies (tomato paste)
**TIP:** Excellent for use with pork or chicken stir fry, meatballs, etc.

## TACO SEASONING

1 ½ T. chili powder
2 T. cumin
1 ½ T. paprika
1 ½ T. onion powder
1 T. garlic powder
1/8 to ½ tsp. cayenne, or to taste

**Directions:**
1. Mix all ingredients together and store in an airtight jar. Recipe makes about 8 tablespoons.

## TERIYAKI SAUCE

**Ingredients:**
1/3 C. soy sauce
3 T. fresh minced ginger (or ½ tsp. ground ginger)
1 T. minced garlic
1 T. Walden Farms balsamic vinegar
8 drops sugar free sweetener, liquid
1 T. olive oil or grapeseed oil

**Directions:**
1. Mix all ingredients together.
2. Heat slightly before using. Store in refrigerator in covered container.

## THAI DRESSING

**Ingredients:**
1 clove garlic, finely chopped
1/8 tsp. ground ginger
3 T. apple cider vinegar
1 tsp. sugar free sweetener, granular

1 tsp. soy sauce
¼ C. olive oil
¼ tsp. crushed red pepper flakes

**Directions:**
1. Combine all ingredients and mix well.
2. Whisk or shake before serving.

## TZATZIKI SAUCE

**Ingredients:**
1 English cucumber, diced
½ C. Walden Farms mayo (any flavor)
¼ tsp. minced garlic
2 ¼ tsp. lemon juice
1 - 2 tsp. chopped fresh dill (or to taste)

**Directions:**
1. In a medium bowl, mix together the mayo, garlic, lemon juice and dill. Fold in cucumber.
2. Refrigerate 2 hours before serving. Store in an airtight container in refrigerator.

**Servings:** Raw cucumbers are unlimited.

# Eggs, Fish & Seafood

**TIP:** A large egg contains 77 calories, with 6 grams of quality protein, 5 grams of fat and trace amounts of carbohydrates. Almost all the nutrients are contained **in the yolk**, the white contains only protein.

Intimidated by cooking or preparing fish or seafood? Not with these recipes. Easy to follow step-by-step instructions to a delicious 'no fail' fish or seafood dish.

**Asian Shrimp Stir Fry**
**Page 56**

**Blackened Grilled Mahi Mahi**
**Page 56**

**Cajun Cauliflower Egg Muffins**
**Page 54**

**Died And Gone To Heaven Oven**
**Omelet - Page 54**

**Scotch Eggs**
**Page 55**

**Grilled Tuna Steak**
**Page 57**

*www.JanevasIdealRecipes.com*

## Egg Recipes

### BACON DEVILED EGGS

**Ingredients:**
6 eggs
2 T. Walden Farms bacon dip
Chopped chives (may use dried), for garnish
Paprika, for garnish
Salt and pepper, to taste

**Directions:**
1. Gently place eggs into a medium sauce pan; add water to cover.
2. Cook on high heat until water comes to a full boil.
3. Turn off burner, cover pan and let eggs sit in water bath for 16 minutes.
4. Drain. Put eggs in ice water for 3-5 minutes. Peel and refrigerate till cooled or cold.
5. Slice eggs lengthwise; give them a gentle squeeze to pop out the yolks. Discard two whole egg yolks which are not to be used in this recipe. (4 whole eggs + 2 egg whites = 8 oz. lean protein.)
6. Place remaining 4 egg yolks in a bowl; add the bacon dip.
7. Mash with a fork; fill the empty egg white halves with the mixture.
8. Sprinkle with chives, paprika (for color) and salt and pepper to taste.

**Servings:** 8 oz. lean protein

### CAJUN CAULIFLOWER EGG MUFFINS

**Ingredients:**
6.5 oz. cauliflower florets (cut in bite size chunks)
2 T. chopped green onions
1 IP omelet mix, any flavor
Cajun or Creole seasoning, to taste
Olive oil cooking spray
Buffalo wing hot sauce, sugar free

**Directions:**
1. Preheat oven to 425 degrees.
2. Spray coat a baking sheet with olive oil spray; lay cauliflower florets on sheet, spreading out evenly. Lightly spray coat the cauliflower florets with olive oil spray.
3. Sprinkle with Cajun or Creole seasoning, to taste.
4. Bake 20 minutes, turning once during baking; set aside.
5. Turn oven down to 350 degrees.
6. Prepare omelet mix according to package directions.
7. Spray coat a regular size muffin tin with cooking spray; pour omelet mix evenly into 3 muffin cups.
8. Add roasted cauliflower evenly and top with green onions.
9. Bake 15 minutes. Serve topped with Buffalo wing hot sauce.

**Servings:** 2 C. veggies + 1 unrestricted

**TIP:** Any prepared veggies may be used. I find that the roasted cauliflower fills the egg muffin cups nicely and almost tastes 'meaty.' Seasonings may be changed to fit personal tastes.

### DIED AND GONE TO HEAVEN OVEN OMELET

**Ingredients:**
2 oz. lean ground beef
Taco Seasoning (to taste), pg. 52
1 C. (3.5 oz.) steamed cauliflower florets
½ C. green bell pepper chunks
½ C. fresh diced tomatoes
1 tsp. olive oil
1 IP omelet mix, any flavor
Salt and pepper, to taste
Garlic powder, to taste
Cooking spray

**Directions:**
1. Preheat oven to 350 degrees.
2. Brown ground beef and add taco seasoning, to taste.
3. In a small skillet, heat olive oil over medium/medium high heat. Add green pepper and sauté until lightly browned and tender. Add tomatoes, and cook 1 additional minute.
4. In a medium bowl, mix taco meat, prepared veggies and omelet mix (prepared according to package directions.) Sprinkle with seasonings.
5. Stir and put into a sprayed individual size casserole dish.
6. Bake 15 minutes or until omelet is set.

**Servings:** 1 unrestricted + 2 oz. lean protein + 2 C. veggies

### EGG SALAD CELERY BOATS

**Ingredients:**
6 eggs
1 T. Dijon or yellow mustard
2 T. Walden Farms mayo (any flavor)
1 - 2 tsp. dill pickle juice
1 T. chopped green onion
Salt, to taste
Lemon pepper, to taste
Celery sticks (unlimited)
Seasoning blend or paprika (for topping)

**Directions:**
1. Gently place eggs into a medium sauce pan; add water to cover.
2. Cook on high heat until water

comes to a full boil.

3. Turn off burner, cover pan and let eggs sit in water bath for 16 minutes.

4. Drain.  Put eggs in ice water for 3-5 minutes.  Peel, discard two egg yolks, and refrigerate till cooled or cold.

5. In a medium bowl, mash eggs with a fork.

6. Add mustard, salt, lemon pepper, mayo, green onion and dill pickle juice.  Mix.

7. Fill celery sticks with egg salad for egg salad celery boats.  Sprinkle with paprika or your favorite seasoning blend.

**Servings:**  8 oz. lean protein (4 whole eggs + 2 egg whites)

**TIP:**  Dip celery sticks into egg salad as an alternative serving suggestion. The egg salad is delicious topped with a Creole or Cajun seasoning blend.

## HONEY DIJON DEVILED EGGS

**Ingredients:**
**6 eggs**
**1 T. Walden Farms mayo (any flavor)**
**1 T. Walden Farms honey Dijon dressing**
**¼ tsp. onion powder**
**¼ tsp. salt**
**Chopped chives (may use dried), for garnish**
**Salt and pepper, to taste**
**Paprika**

**Directions:**
1. Gently place eggs into a medium sauce pan; add water to cover.
2. Cook on high heat until water comes to a full boil.
3. Turn off burner, cover pan and let eggs sit in water bath for 16 minutes.
4. Drain.  Put eggs in ice water for 3-5 minutes.  Peel and refrigerate till cooled or cold.
5. Slice eggs lengthwise; give them a gentle squeeze to pop out the yolks. Discard two whole egg yolks which are not to be used in this recipe.

(4 whole eggs + 2 egg whites = 8 oz. lean protein.)

6. Place remaining 4 egg yolks in a bowl; add the mayo, honey Dijon dressing, onion powder, salt and a pinch of paprika.  Mash together; fill egg white halves with mixture.

7. Sprinkle with paprika, chives and black pepper to taste.

**Servings:**  8 oz. lean protein (4 whole eggs + 2 egg whites)

## ITALIAN HERBED EGGS WITH TOMATOES

**Ingredients:**
**4 eggs + 2 egg whites, lightly beaten together**
**1 C. canned diced tomatoes, drained (reserving 3 T. juice)**
**¼ tsp. salt**
**¼ tsp. Italian seasoning**
**2 tsp. extra virgin olive oil**

**Directions:**
1.  Heat oil in a large skillet over medium heat.
2.  Add eggs, salt and Italian seasoning.  Using a spatula, scramble and cook until halfway done; add tomatoes and reserved juice.
3.  Continue to cook until heated through and eggs are firm.

**Servings:**  8 oz. lean protein + 1 1/2 C veggies (1C. canned tomatoes = 1 1/2 C. fresh)

## OMELET BAGELS

**Ingredients:**
**1 IP omelet mix (dry), any flavor**
**4 oz. water**
**1 oz. milk**
**½ C. Pico de Gallo Salsa, pg. 50**
**Hot sauce, optional**
**Cooking spray**

**Directions:**
1. Preheat oven to 350 degrees.
2. Shake or whisk together the

omelet mix, water and milk.

3. Spray a donut pan and evenly pour the omelet mix into the pan making 3 omelet bagels.

4. Bake 10 minutes.

5. To serve, top with salsa and/or hot sauce.

**Servings:**  1 unrestricted + ½ C. veggies

**TIP:**  Serve sandwiched with roasted veggies, sliced tomatoes and/or lean protein, etc. for a tasty breakfast sandwich.  Great for on the go!

## SCOTCH EGGS

**Ingredients:**
**2 hard boiled eggs, peeled**
**4 oz. lean ground chicken (or other lean ground protein)**
**1 tsp. Sausage Seasoning, pg. 51**
**Salt and pepper, to taste**
**Olive oil spray**

**Directions:**
1. Preheat oven to 375 degrees.
2. In a small bowl, combine chicken and Sausage Seasoning.
3. Make into two patties; wrap each egg with a patty and seal.
4. Spray a baking sheet with olive oil and place eggs on sheet.
5. Bake 22 - 25 minutes or until deep golden brown.
6. Season with salt and pepper, to taste.  May be eaten hot or cold; keep refrigerated if storing.

**Servings:**  2 eggs = 8 oz. lean protein

**TIP:**  Perfect for a meal on the go when prepared ahead.

## TACO CASSEROLE BRUNCH BAKE

**Ingredients:**
2 oz. lean ground beef
Taco Seasoning (to taste), pg. 52
½ C. broccoli florets, steamed
½ C. cauliflower florets, steamed
1 IP omelet mix, any flavor
Salt and pepper, to taste
Cooking spray

**Directions:**
1. Preheat oven to 350 degrees.
2. In a skillet over medium/medium high heat brown the ground beef seasoned with taco seasoning; drain any fat and set aside.
3. Layer steamed vegetables in a sprayed single serving baking dish.
4. Layer browned taco meat evenly over veggies.
5. Prepare omelet mix according to package directions. Pour over meat and veggies.
6. Bake 10 minutes.

**Servings:** 1 unrestricted + 2 oz. lean protein + 1 C. veggies

**TIP:** I store previously steamed veggies in the refrigerator to have on hand for dishes like this.

## Fish & Seafood Recipes

## ASIAN SHRIMP STIR FRY
*With Shirataki Noodles*

**Ingredients:**
1 lb. shrimp, thawed (cooked, deveined, tails off)
2 T. Walden Farms Asian dressing
1 T. + 1 tsp. soy sauce
2 tsp. Walden Farms orange marmalade
1 T. olive oil
1 C. shirataki noodles or 1 C. zoodles, pg. 95

1 ½ C. broccoli florets
1 C. sliced baby bella mushrooms
¼ C. diced green pepper
2 tsp. minced garlic
2 T. chopped fresh cilantro
2 slices jicama (cut to the thickness of a water chestnut slice)
4 T. chicken broth (fat free, low sodium), divided

**Directions:**
1. Pour shirataki noodles into a strainer and rinse well with cold water (they have an earthy smell when the pouch is opened.) Set aside.
2. Cut two slices jicama the thickness of a water chestnut. Place slices on a work surface and press melon baller onto the slices to cut out circular discs (they will look and taste like water chestnuts in this dish.)
3. In a small bowl, mix together the Asian dressing, soy sauce, orange marmalade and garlic. Heat in the microwave about 30 seconds. Stir mixture; set aside.
4. Place shrimp in a bowl; pour Asian dressing mixture over shrimp. Toss and set aside.
5. Heat olive oil in a wok or skillet over medium/medium high heat; add broccoli and green pepper. Stir fry 8 - 10 minutes.
6. Add mushrooms and 2 T. chicken broth; stir fry an additional 3 - 5 minutes. Add remaining chicken broth during cooking as necessary.
7. Add shrimp mixture and jicama 'water chestnuts' to the pan; stir fry one minute. Add the shirataki or zucchini noodles and toss until heated through.
8. Remove from heat. Toss in cilantro and serve.

**Servings:** Entire recipe = 16 oz. lean protein + 4 C. veggies; ½ recipe = 8 oz. lean protein + 2 C. veggies

**Tip:** Be sure to add zoodle veggie count, if using.

## BLACKENED GRILLED MAHI MAHI
*Delicious served with Mango Salsa (pg. 49) and Coconut Lime Cauliflower Rice (pg. 90)*

**Ingredients:**
1 - 8 oz. Mahi Mahi fillet
Cajun or Creole seasoning, to taste
1 - 2 tsp. olive oil

**Directions:**
1. Pat Mahi fillets dry with a paper towel. Sprinkle both sides of fillets with seasoning of choice.
2. Add 1 - 2 tsp. olive oil to a grill fry pan. Heat on medium/medium high heat.
3. When oil is hot, add Mahi fillets; cook 3 minutes on each side or until fish flakes easily with a fork.

**Servings:** 8 oz. lean protein

**TIP:** Seasonings of choice may be substituted for the Cajun or Creole seasoning. As an alternative option to the regular olive oil, I use butter flavored olive oil for this dish. I also use an olive oil mister to spray the pan to ensure the 1 -2 tsp. of olive oil covers the entire bottom of pan; spray the tops of the fillets before turning.

## CAJUN SHRIMP ALFREDO & ZOODLES

**Ingredients:**
10.5 oz. (3 C.) cauliflower florets
1 tsp. minced garlic
¾ C. + 2 T. water
Salt and pepper, to taste
Garlic powder, to taste

**Cajun seasoning (sugar free), to taste**
**2 tsp. olive oil, divided**
**8 oz. shrimp, thawed (cooked, deveined, tails off)**
**1 ½ C. zoodles (spiralized zucchini noodles)**
**Olive oil cooking spray**

**Directions:**
1. Cut cauliflower florets into chunks about the size of cherry tomatoes; set aside.
2. In a medium sauce pan, heat 1 tsp. olive oil over medium heat; add minced garlic and cook until fragrant but not browned.
3. Add the water and cauliflower florets to the sauce pan and bring to a boil. (The water won't cover the cauliflower but that's okay.) Once the water boils, reduce heat to medium/medium low; cover sauce pan and continue to simmer 8 - 10 minutes or until cauliflower is fork tender.
4. Meanwhile, spiralize a zucchini until you have 1 ½ C. zoodles; set aside.
5. Heat 1 tsp. olive oil in a skillet over medium/medium high heat. Add thawed shrimp seasoned with garlic powder and Cajun seasoning; stir fry until heated through. Set aside and keep warm.
6. Transfer the entire contents of the sauce pan into a blender or food processor. Season with salt and pepper; blend until creamy smooth. (Be careful with hot mixtures when blending; they can blow the top off a blender. I place a towel over the lid and hold down while blending; use a bullet style blender to eliminate this issue.)
7. Heat a skillet on medium/medium high heat; spray with olive oil cooking

spray. Add zoodles, spraying lightly with olive oil cooking spray and season with garlic powder. Stir fry just until heated through, about one minute; do not overcook the zoodles or they will become mushy.
8. Plate the zoodles; top with cauliflower Alfredo mixture and shrimp. Season with salt and pepper.

**Servings:** Entire recipe = 8 oz. lean protein + 4 C. veggies (cauliflower + zoodles.) The cauliflower Alfredo sauce adds 3 C. to the dish; the entire amount is not needed. I use about 1/6 of the entire sauce recipe to top the zoodles. The entire dish would then equal 8 oz. lean protein + 2 C. veggies. Store the remaining Alfredo sauce in the refrigerator for another meal or recipe.

# GRILLED TUNA STEAK
*Only six minutes to a delicious meal*

**Ingredients:**
**1 - 8 oz. tuna steak**
**¼ C. lemon juice**
**1 T. olive oil**
**1 tsp. minced garlic**
**¼ tsp. salt**
**¼ tsp. ground ginger**
**1 tsp. soy sauce**
**Olive oil cooking spray**

**Directions:**
1. Mix all ingredients together except tuna steak. Pour into a large resealable baggie and add tuna steak. Close bag tightly, releasing any air out of the bag. Refrigerate ½ - 4 hours to marinate the steak.
2. Heat a frying pan (I use a grill type frying pan) sprayed with 1 tsp. olive oil cooking spray over medium high heat. Oil is hot when a drop of water

sizzles when added. (The tsp. of sprayed olive oil is in addition to the 1 T. olive oil listed in the ingredients).
3. When the frying pan is hot, remove the tuna steak from marinade; add the tuna steak to the pan. A sizzling sound should be heard. Fry 3 minutes, uncovered.
4. Turn tuna steak over; fry an additional 3 minutes, uncovered. Serve hot or cold. Discard marinade.

**Servings:** 8 oz. lean protein

**TIP:** Since the marinade is discarded, there is no need to be concerned with the 1 T. of olive oil in the ingredients; most of it will be discarded and will not be consumed. I estimate 1 tsp. olive oil from the marinade will be on the tuna steak. The tuna may be raw to well done depending on personal preference. A larger tuna steak, cooked 3 minutes per side, will be cooked to medium with a small amount of pink in the middle. Adjust cooking time as necessary. Steaks may be cooked on a BBQ grill instead of on the stove top.

# ITALIAN FISH FILLETS

**Ingredients:**
**1 lb. fish fillets**
**8 oz. can tomato sauce (no added sugar)**
**2 tsp. olive oil**
**1 tsp. Walden Farms Italian dressing or apple cider vinegar**
**¼ tsp. salt**
**¼ tsp. garlic powder**
**1/8 tsp. black pepper**
**½ tsp. minced garlic**
**Chopped fresh parsley, for garnish**
**Cooking spray**

**Directions:**
1. Preheat oven to 375 degrees.
2. In a bowl, combine all ingredients except fish and parsley. Whisk together.
3. Spray a 9"x 9" baking dish or size needed to accommodate fish fillets. Pour ½ the sauce into the baking

dish.

4. Arrange fish fillets over sauce; top with remaining sauce.

5. Bake uncovered 20 minutes or until fish flakes easily with a fork.

6. Serve garnished with chopped fresh parsley.

**Servings:** Entire recipe = 16 oz. lean protein + 2 cup veggies; ½ recipe = 8 oz. lean protein + 1 C. veggies

**TIP:** This dish is delicious served with Roasted Fennel and Red Cabbage Slaw; recipe pg. 93. Two cups tomatoes cooked down to a sauce = approximately 1 cup. This conversion was considered in the veggie count.

## ORANGE STIR FRY

*This recipe submitted by Steven Larry*

**Ingredients:**
2 C. assorted veggies (broccoli, asparagus, celery and mushrooms)
8 oz. chicken, shrimp, tilapia or salmon; cooked, bite sized
2 - 3 T. Walden Farms orange marmalade
Sea salt, to taste
Pepper, to taste
Garlic powder, to taste
Onion powder, to taste
Chopped fresh cilantro, to taste (optional)
2 tsp. olive oil or grapeseed oil

**Directions:**
1. Stir fry assorted veggies in olive oil or grapeseed oil. Add mushrooms toward end of cooking time.
2. Add cooked, bite size chicken, shrimp, tilapia or salmon. Mix and stir in orange marmalade. Season with sea salt, pepper, garlic powder, onion powder and cilantro, to taste.

**Servings:** 8 oz. lean protein + 2 C. veggies.

## PERFECT SALMON Every Time

**Ingredients:**
8 oz. salmon fillet
Olive oil (I prefer using an olive oil mister)
Salt and pepper, to taste
Other seasonings of choice (optional)

**Directions:**
1. Spray the salmon fillet with olive oil and sprinkle with salt and pepper and/or other seasonings, to taste.
2. Place salmon in a cold oven (skin side down unless salmon is skinless) on a baking sheet lightly sprayed with olive oil.
3. Turn on oven to 400 degrees; bake 25 minutes. The salmon comes out tender, moist and flaky - absolutely perfect. A no-fail method.

**Servings:** 8 oz. lean protein

## PERFECTLY SEARED SCALLOPS

**Ingredients:**
8 oz. sea scallops, medium to large size
1 T. olive oil
Sea salt, to taste
Freshly ground black pepper, to taste
Garlic powder, to taste
Lemon for squeezing (optional)

**Directions:**
1. Remove tiny side muscle from scallops if necessary. Rinse scallops with cold water and pat dry with paper towel.
2. Add oil to a large frying pan. Heat over high heat.
3. Season scallops with salt, pepper and garlic powder. When the oil in the frying pan begins to smoke, add the scallops making sure they are not touching.
4. Sear scallops 1 ½ minutes on each side; do not touch them while they are searing. Squeeze lemon juice over scallops if desired. Serve immediately.

**Servings:** 8 oz. lean protein

## SHRIMP CEVICHE

**Ingredients:**
1 lb. shrimp, thawed (cooked, deveined, tails off)
1 ½ C. diced tomato
¼ C. chopped green onion
¼ C. chopped fresh cilantro
Juice of 1 lime
1 T. lemon juice
½ C. diced yellow onion
1 ½ tsp. minced Anaheim chile pepper
¼ tsp. salt, or to taste
Black pepper, to taste
1 ½ C. cucumber slices, cut ¼" thick

**Directions:**
1. Cut the cooked shrimp in small chunks (make sure it is cool); place in a medium sized bowl.
2. Add remaining ingredients except cucumber. Gently mix together.
3. Serve ceviche cold on top of cucumber slices.

**Servings:** Entire recipe = 16 oz. lean protein + 4 C. veggies; ½ recipe = 8 oz. lean protein + 2 C. veggies.

**TIP:** Keep ceviche refrigerated until ready to eat. Perfect for cold snacking or bringing to an event.

## SHRIMP COCKTAIL

**Ingredients:**
8 oz. shrimp, thawed (cooked, deveined, tails on)
1/3 C. Walden Farms ketchup
Horseradish, to taste
Lemon juice, to taste
Hot sauce, to taste

**Directions:**
1. In a bowl, combine all ingredients except shrimp; stir to mix. Serve with chilled shrimp.

**Servings:** 8 oz. lean protein

## SOFRITO SHRIMP
*A popular Puerto Rican dish*

**Ingredients:**
16 oz. raw medium size shrimp, deveined and tails off
½ tsp. garlic powder
Salt & pepper, to taste
½ C. Sofrito, recipe pg. 51
½ C. tomato sauce
1 T. olive oil
Chopped fresh cilantro or green onion, to taste (optional)

**Directions:**
1. In a medium bowl, stir together the sofrito and tomato sauce; set aside.
2. In a large frying pan, heat olive oil over medium high heat. Add shrimp and season with garlic powder, salt and pepper; stir fry 3-4 minutes or until shrimp is pink all the way through.
3. Turn down heat to medium/medium low; add sofrito mixture and continue to simmer 3-4 minutes, stirring often.
4. Plate and sprinkle with cilantro or green onion, if using.

**Servings:** Entire recipe = 16 oz. lean protein + 1 ½ C. veggies (sofrito + tomato sauce equivalent); ½ recipe = 8 oz. lean protein + ¾ C. veggies

**TIP:** Delicious served over cauliflower rice or zoodles.

## SPICY TUNA ROTINI

**Ingredients:**
1 IP plain rotini, cooked and cooled
2 oz. albacore white tuna (canned in water, drained)
½ C. chopped celery
½ C. chopped tomato
½ C. chopped onion
½ C. chopped green bell pepper
1 T. Walden Farms mayo (any flavor)
¼ tsp. Cajun seasoning

**Directions:**
1. In a bowl, mix together all ingredients.

**Servings:** 1 unrestricted + 2 oz. lean protein + 2 C. veggies.

## TARRAGON DIJON GLAZED SALMON
*Easy and incredibly delicious*

**Ingredients:**
2 – 8 oz. salmon filets (skin on or off)
Creole or Cajun seasoning, to taste
Salt and pepper, to taste
4 tsp. Dijon mustard
2 T. Walden Farms or IP pancake syrup
¼ tsp. onion powder
1 T. chopped fresh tarragon leaves (or 1 tsp. dried tarragon)
2 tsp. extra virgin olive oil
2 C. fresh spinach
Olive oil cooking spray

**Directions:**
1. Do not preheat oven, you will be placing salmon in a cold oven.
2. Place salmon skin side down on a sprayed baking sheet (or line with parchment paper).
3. Season with salt, pepper and Creole or Cajun seasoning.
4. In a small bowl, mix together the Dijon, pancake syrup, onion powder and tarragon.
5. Spread mustard mixture evenly over salmon filets.
6. Place salmon in a cold oven, turn on oven to 400 degrees.
7. Bake 25 minutes.
8. While salmon is baking, toss spinach with the extra virgin olive oil.
9. Plate spinach; serve salmon on top.

**Servings:** Entire recipe = 16 oz. lean protein; ½ recipe = 8 oz. lean protein
NOTE: You will not need to count the raw spinach, it is unlimited.

**TIP:** Spritz the salmon with the olive oil cooking spray to give it a nice shine before serving.

# Pancakes, Waffles, French Toast & Donuts

"Waffles are just pancakes with abs."
Unknown

"Eat Breakfast like a King, Lunch like a Prince, Dinner like a Pauper."
Adelle Davies

"Honey comes from bees,
Apples from trees,
But pancakes come from heaven."
Unknown

**Chocolate Chip Zucchini Waffles**
**Page 62**

**Chocolate Fruit Waffles**
**Page 62**

**French Toast**
**Page 63**

**Gingerbread Chocolate Chip**
**Waffle - Page 63**

**Bakery Shoppe Donuts**
**Page 61**

**Cinnamon Zucchini Waffles**
**Page 63**

## APPLE FRITTER WAFFLE

**Ingredients:**
1 IP chocolatey caramel mug cake mix (dry)
¼ C. Caramel Fried Apples, pg. 38; or Zucchini Fried Apples, pg. 46
2 T. water
Cooking spray

**Directions:**
1. In a medium size bowl, combine all ingredients; stir to mix.
2. Bake waffle in a sprayed waffle maker according to manufacturer directions.

**Servings:** 1 unrestricted + ½ C. veggies (¼ C. cooked 'apples' is the estimated equivalent to ½ C. raw 'apples')

## BAKERY SHOPPE DONUTS
*Lemon, strawberry, orange or triple chocolate donuts*
*Loaded with chocolate chunks*

**Ingredients:**
1 package (2 squares) IP lemon, strawberry, orange or triple chocolate wafers (crushed)
1 IP chocolate chip pancake mix (dry)
1 tsp. baking powder
1 large egg, lightly beaten
¼ C. water
Cooking spray

**Directions:**
1. Preheat oven to 350 degrees.
2. In a medium bowl, mix dry ingredients.
3. Add liquid ingredients; stir to mix.
4. Generously spray a standard size donut pan; pour batter into pan making 6 donuts.

---

5. Bake 8 minutes.

**Servings:** 6 donuts =
2 unrestricted + 2 oz. lean protein;
3 donuts =
1 unrestricted + 1 oz. lean protein

## BANANAS FOSTER WAFFLES

**Ingredients:**
1 IP plain pancake mix (dry)
1 IP vanilla pudding mix (dry)
1 tsp. baking powder
4 T. liquid egg whites
2 T. Walden Farms caramel syrup
4 T. water
1/8 tsp. banana extract
1/8 tsp. rum extract
Cooking spray

**Directions:**
1. In a medium bowl, mix together dry ingredients. Add liquid ingredients; stir to mix.
2. Coat heated waffle iron with cooking spray before adding waffle batter; bake according to manufacturer directions making 4 waffles.
3. Serve with a mix of warmed Walden Farms caramel and pancake syrup, if desired.

**Servings:** Entire recipe
= 2 unrestricted; ½ recipe
= 1 unrestricted

## BLUEBERRY PANCAKES

**Ingredients:**
1 IP plain pancake mix (dry)
¼ tsp. baking powder
3 T. Walden Farms blueberry syrup
2 T. liquid egg whites
Cooking spray

---

**Directions:**
1. In a small bowl, mix dry ingredients together. Add liquid ingredients; stir to mix.
2. Coat a frying pan with cooking spray; heat on medium. Pour batter into frying pan to make 2 pancakes; lightly spread batter into circles to make equal sized pancakes.
3. Cook until edges start to look dry or underside is golden brown. This will take about 2 minutes on medium heat. Flip and cook other side, about 30 seconds.
4. Serve with warmed Walden Farms blueberry syrup.

**Servings:** 1 unrestricted

## CHOCOLATE BROWNIE WAFFLE

**Ingredients:**
1 IP chocolatey caramel mug cake mix (dry)
2 T. Walden Farms chocolate syrup
2 T. water
Cooking spray

**Directions:**
1. In a medium size bowl, mix all ingredients.
2. Bake waffles in a sprayed waffle maker according to manufacturer directions.
3. Serve with additional warmed Walden Farms chocolate syrup and/or pancake syrup, or store cooled waffles in a baggie and take with you on the go. No syrup needed.

**Servings:** 1 unrestricted

# CHOCOLATE CANDY CANE DONUTS

**Ingredients:** (donuts)
1 IP dark chocolate pudding mix (dry)
1 IP chocolate chip pancake mix (dry)
1 tsp. baking powder
1 tsp. sugar free sweetener, granular
1/3 C. liquid egg whites
2 tsp. olive oil
1 tsp. *fudge brownie flavor fountain, optional
1/8 tsp. peppermint extract
4 T. water
Cooking spray

**Directions:**
1. Preheat oven to 350 degrees.
2. In a medium bowl, mix together the dry ingredients.
3. Add liquid ingredients; stir to mix.
4. Spray a regular size donut pan with cooking spray; spoon batter into donut pan making 4 donuts.
5. Bake 8-10 minutes; cool.
6. Top with drizzle (recipe below), optional.

**Ingredients:** (drizzle)
2 T. Walden Farms marshmallow dip
Red food coloring

**Directions:**
1. Divide marshmallow dip equally into two separate bowls.
2. Add red food coloring to one bowl, enough drops to achieve desired color.
3. Using a fork, whisk each bowl of dip separately until smooth.
4. Drizzle donuts with alternating crisscross pattern.

**Servings:** 4 donuts = 2 unrestricted; 2 donuts = 1 unrestricted

**TIP:** *You may purchase the fudge brownie flavor fountain at www.olivenation.com; it is optional but provides a fudge-like texture and flavor.

# CHOCOLATE CHIP ZUCCHINI WAFFLES

**Ingredients:**
1 IP chocolate chip pancake mix (dry)
1 tsp. baking powder
1 tsp. sugar free sweetener, granular
½ tsp. cinnamon
2 T. + 1 tsp. liquid egg whites
2 tsp. Walden Farms pancake or chocolate syrup (or water)
½ tsp. vanilla extract
¼ C. shredded zucchini
Cooking spray

**Directions:**
1. Place shredded zucchini in a small bowl; microwave for 30 seconds. Remove and blot well with paper towels to absorb moisture.
2. In a medium bowl, mix together the dry ingredients. Add liquid ingredients; stir to mix. Fold in zucchini.
3. Spray heated waffle iron with cooking spray before adding waffle batter; bake according to manufacturer directions.
4. Serve with Walden Farms syrup.

**Servings:** 1 unrestricted + 1/4 C. veggies

# CHOCOLATE FRUIT WAFFLES

**Ingredients:**
1 IP chocolatey caramel mug cake mix (dry)

1/3 C. Strawberry Rhubarb Compote, pg. 45; divided
1 T. water
Walden Farms chocolate syrup (for topping)
Cooking spray

**Directions:**
1. Preheat waffle iron.
2. In a medium bowl, combine mug cake mix, 2 T. compote mixture and water; mix to form a thick batter.
3. Bake waffles in a sprayed waffle maker according to manufacturer directions.
4. Top with the remaining compote mixture and drizzle with warmed Walden Farms chocolate syrup.

**Servings:** 1 unrestricted + ½ C. veggies. (1/3 C. strawberry rhubarb compote = ½ C. veggies)

# CHOCOLATE PEANUT BUTTER CUP WAFFLES

**Ingredients:**
1 IP milk or dark chocolate pudding mix (dry)
1 tsp. baking powder
2 T. + 1 tsp. liquid egg whites
2 T. Walden Farms peanut butter
3 T. water
Cooking spray

**Directions:**
1. In a medium bowl, mix together the milk chocolate pudding mix and baking powder. Add egg whites,

peanut butter and water; stir to mix. Batter will be thick.

2. Spray heated waffle iron before baking; cook according to manufacturer directions making 1 - 2 waffles.

3. Serve with Peanut Syrup, optional.

**PEANUT SYRUP:** Mix together 1 T. Walden Farms maple syrup, 1 tsp. Walden Farms peanut butter and ¼ tsp. vanilla extract. Heat 15 seconds on high in microwave; stir to mix. Pour over waffles.

Servings: 1 unrestricted

## CINNAMON ZUCCHINI WAFFLES

Ingredients:
1 IP plain pancake mix (dry)
1 tsp. baking powder
1 tsp. sugar free sweetener, granular
½ tsp. cinnamon
2 T. + 1 tsp. liquid egg whites
2 tsp. water
½ tsp. vanilla extract
¼ C. shredded zucchini
Cooking spray

Directions:
1. Place shredded zucchini in a small bowl; microwave on high for 30 seconds. Remove from microwave and blot with paper towels to absorb moisture.
2. In a medium bowl, mix together the dry ingredients. Add liquid ingredients; stir to mix. Fold in zucchini.
3. Spray heated waffle iron with cooking spray; add waffle batter. Bake according to manufacturer directions making 1 -2 waffles.
4. Serve with Walden Farms syrup.

Servings: 1 unrestricted + 1/4 C. veggies

## DOUBLE CHOCOLATE CHIP ZUCCHINI WAFFLES

Ingredients:
1 IP milk or dark chocolate pudding mix (dry)
1 IP chocolate chip pancake mix (dry)
¼ tsp. baking powder
¼ C. liquid egg whites
2 T. Walden Farms chocolate syrup
3 T. water
¼ tsp. vanilla extract
½ C. shredded zucchini
Cooking spray

Directions:
1. Place shredded zucchini in a small bowl; microwave for 30 seconds. Remove and blot well with paper towels to absorb moisture.
2. In a medium bowl, mix together the dry ingredients. Add liquid ingredients; stir to mix. Fold in zucchini.
3. Spray heated waffle iron with cooking spray before adding waffle batter; bake according to manufacturer directions making 2 - 4 waffles.
4. Serve with a combination of Walden Farms pancake and chocolate syrup.

Servings: Entire recipe = 2 unrestricted + 1/2 C. veggies; ½ recipe = 1 unrestricted + 1/4 C. veggies

**TIP:** Store in refrigerator or freeze. Pop into the toaster to reheat.

## FRENCH TOAST

Ingredients:
1 recipe muffin loaf bread of choice (recipes in Breads, Muffins & Wraps Section)
2 T. liquid egg whites
Cooking spray
Walden Farms syrup

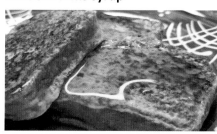

Directions:
1. Using ½ the muffin loaf bread, cut into 3 equal slices.
2. Place 2 T. liquid egg whites in a small shallow bowl.
3. Dip the 3 slices of bread into the egg whites, coating both sides.
4. Preheat a skillet over medium/medium high heat; spray with cooking spray.
5. Place bread slices in heated skillet; cook until lightly browned on both sides, pressing down firmly on each slice with a spatula during cooking.
6. Serve with Walden Farms syrup.

Servings: 3 slices = 1 unrestricted (if using an unrestricted muffin bread recipe)

## GINGERBREAD CHOCOLATE CHIP WAFFLE

Ingredients:
1 IP chocolatey caramel mug cake mix (dry)
½ tsp. cinnamon
Pinch ground cloves
Pinch ground ginger
Pinch nutmeg
2 T. Walden Farms caramel syrup
2 T. water
Cooking spray

**Directions:**
1. In a medium size bowl, mix all dry ingredients; add liquid ingredients. Stir to mix.
2. Bake waffle(s) in a sprayed waffle maker according to manufacturer directions.
3. Serve with Walden Farms pancake syrup, or store cooled in a baggie and take with you on the go; no syrup needed.

**Servings:** 1 unrestricted

## LEMON CHOCOLATE CHIP WAFFLES

**Ingredients:**
1 IP vanilla pudding mix (dry)
1 IP chocolate chip pancake mix (dry)
¼ tsp. baking powder
¼ C. liquid egg whites
3 T. water
½ tsp. lemon extract
Cooking spray

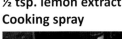

**Directions:**
1. In a medium sized bowl mix together the dry ingredients. Add liquid ingredients; stir to mix.
2. Spray heated waffle iron with cooking spray before adding waffle batter. Bake according to manufacturer directions making 2 - 4 waffles. Continue to spray waffle iron before adding batter for each baked waffle.
3. Serve with warmed Walden Farms

chocolate and/or pancake syrup.

**Servings:** Entire recipe
= 2 unrestricted; ½ recipe
= 1 unrestricted

**TIP:** Refrigerate any remaining waffles in a baggie. Pop in the toaster to reheat.

## MOCHA WAFFLES

**Ingredients:**
1 IP cappuccino drink mix (dry)
1 IP chocolate chip pancake mix (dry)
¼ tsp. baking powder
¼ C. liquid egg whites
2 T. water (or cold coffee)
½ tsp. vanilla or coffee extract
1 T. Walden Farms chocolate syrup
Cooking spray

**Directions:**
1. In a medium size bowl mix together the dry ingredients. Add liquid ingredients; stir to mix.
2. Spray heated waffle iron with cooking spray before adding waffle batter. Bake according to manufacturer directions making 2 - 4 waffles. Continue to spray waffle iron before adding batter for each baked waffle.
3. Serve with warmed Walden Farms chocolate and/or pancake syrup.

**Servings:** Entire recipe
= 2 unrestricted; ½ recipe
= 1 unrestricted

**TIP:** Refrigerate any remaining waffles in a baggie. Pop in the toaster to reheat.

## PANCAKES (BASIC RECIPE)

**Ingredients:**
1 IP crispy cereal (dry), crushed (or IP apple or maple oatmeal mix, dry)
¼ tsp. baking powder
½ tsp. sugar free sweetener, granular
¼ tsp cinnamon
1/3 C. liquid egg whites
¼ tsp. vanilla extract
Cooking spray

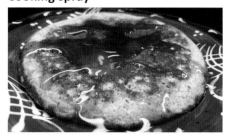

**Directions:**
1. Mix together dry ingredients in a medium bowl. Add liquid ingredients; stir to mix.
2. Spray a small frying pan with cooking spray; heat on medium. Pour batter into frying pan making 1 pancake; cook both sides until golden brown.
3. Serve with Walden Farms syrup.

**Servings:** 1 unrestricted

## PEANUT BUTTER WAFFLES

**Ingredients:**
1 IP crispy cereal packet (dry), crushed
1 tsp. baking powder
1 tsp. sugar free sweetener, granular
2 T. + 1 tsp. liquid egg whites
1 T. Walden Farms peanut butter
Cooking spray

**Directions:**
1. In a medium size bowl, mix together the dry ingredients. Add liquid ingredients; stir to mix.
2. Spray heated waffle iron with cooking spray before adding waffle batter. Bake according to manufacturer directions making 1 - 2 waffles. Continue to spray waffle iron before adding batter for each baked waffle.
3. Serve with Peanut Syrup, optional.

**PEANUT SYRUP:** Mix together 1 T. Walden Farms pancake syrup, 1 tsp. Walden Farms peanut butter and ¼ tsp. vanilla extract. Heat 15 seconds on high in microwave; stir to mix. Pour over waffles.

**Servings:** 1 unrestricted

## SALTED CARAMEL CHOCOLATE CHIP PANCAKES

**Ingredients:**
1 IP chocolate chip pancake mix, dry
¼ tsp. baking powder
Pinch of IP salt
2 T. Walden Farms caramel syrup
2 T. liquid egg whites
1 T. water
Cooking spray

**Directions:**
1. In a medium bowl, mix together the dry ingredients. Add liquid ingredients; stir to mix.
2. Spray a frying pan with cooking spray and heat on medium. Pour batter into frying pan making 2 pancakes; lightly spread batter out into circles making pancakes of equal size.
3. Cook until edges start to look dry or underside is golden brown. This will take about 2 minutes on medium heat. Flip and cook other side about 30 seconds.
4. Serve with warmed Walden Farms caramel syrup.

**Servings:** 1 unrestricted

## STRAWBERRY CHOCOLATE CHIP PANCAKES

**Ingredients:**
1 IP chocolate chip pancake mix (dry)
¼ tsp. baking powder
2 T. Walden Farms strawberry syrup
2 T. liquid egg whites
1 T. water
Cooking spray

**Directions:**
1. Mix dry ingredients in a small bowl. Add liquid ingredients; stir to mix.
2. Coat a frying pan with cooking spray and heat on medium. Pour batter into frying pan making 2 pancakes; lightly spread batter out into circles making pancakes of equal size.
3. Cook until edges start to look dry or underside is golden brown. This will take about 2 minutes over medium heat. Flip and cook other side about 30 seconds.
4. Serve with warmed additional Walden Farms strawberry syrup.

**Servings:** 1 unrestricted

## STRAWBERRY CHOCOLATE CHIP WAFFLES

**Ingredients:**
1 IP chocolate chip pancake mix (dry)
1 tsp. baking powder
2 T. liquid egg whites
1 T. + ½ tsp. Walden Farms strawberry syrup
Cooking spray

**Directions:**
1. In a medium bowl, mix together the dry ingredients. Add liquid ingredients; stir to mix. Batter will be thick.
2. Spray heated waffle iron; bake according to manufacturer directions making 1 - 2 waffles.
3. Serve with warmed additional Walden Farms strawberry syrup.

**Servings:** 1 unrestricted

## THE PERFECT CHOCOLATE CHIP PANCAKE

**Ingredients:**
1 IP chocolate chip pancake mix (dry)
3 T. liquid egg whites
¼ tsp. cinnamon (optional)
Cooking spray

**Directions:**
1. In a small bowl, mix together the dry pancake mix and cinnamon. Add liquid egg whites; stir to mix.
2. Preheat a frying pan just below medium heat.
3. Coat the frying pan with cooking spray; add pancake batter and spread into a 6" circle with the back of a sprayed spoon.
4. Cook until the edge starts to look dry and bubbles start to pop.
5. Flip the pancake and cook until lightly browned; it will not take long on the second side.

**Servings:** 1 unrestricted

**TIP:** Refrain from flipping the pancake too soon or it will be a mess. The key to this pancake recipe is cooking at a lower temperature and having patience. At the lower temperature, it will take longer to cook than the average pancake. The pancake is thick but light and fluffy.

# Poultry Main Dishes

**TIP:** If you're looking for a quick and nutritious meal, a juicy and delicious chicken breast can be cooked in 6 minutes. Butterfly the chicken breast and season with your favorite spice blend; heat 2 teaspoons olive oil in a frying pan over medium/medium high heat. When the frying pan is hot, place chicken in the pan and cook each side 3 minutes. For more tips and techniques for butterflying a chicken breast, go to www.JanevasIdealRecipes.com.

**Bruschetta Chicken**
Page 67

**Buffalo Chicken Meatballs**
Page 68

**Orange Chicken**
Page 71

**Chicken & Spinach Pizza Skillet**
Page 69

**Turkey Zoodle Egg Bake**
Page 73

**White Cheddar Chicken Fingers**
Page 73

## BACON SPINACH MUSHROOM STUFFED CHICKEN BREASTS

**Ingredients:**
**2 - 8 oz. chicken breasts (boneless and skinless)**
**1 - 2 tsp. olive oil (using an olive oil mister or spray type oil)**
**1 tsp. minced garlic**
**½ C. chopped green onion**
**1 ½ C. sliced fresh mushrooms**
**2 C. fresh spinach**
**1 T. Walden Farms bacon dip**
**Salt and pepper, to taste**
**Onion powder, to taste**

**Directions:**
1. Heat a medium frying pan on medium/medium high heat; spray mist with olive oil. Add garlic and mushrooms; stir fry until mushrooms start to brown. Keep spraying oil as necessary to keep mushrooms from drying out in the pan.
2. When mushrooms start to turn brown, add green onion and spinach; season with salt, pepper and onion powder, to taste. Stir fry until spinach shrinks down and wilts a bit, spraying oil as necessary. Remove from heat and place mixture on a cutting board.
3. Chop mixture in small pieces with a knife, or pulse through a food processor until chopped, not pureed. Place mixture in a bowl and stir in the bacon dip; set aside.
4. Prepare chicken breasts by placing one hand on top of a breast; slice the chicken horizontally across the center being careful not to cut all the way through. Leave equal thickness on top and bottom of breast; this creates a pocket.

5. Spoon veggie mixture equally into each chicken breast pocket, and press down firmly to 'close' the pocket. Pierce toothpicks through the pocket opening to keep it closed (I use 3 or 4 toothpicks per breast.)
6. Heat a medium frying pan on medium/medium high heat; spray mist with olive oil. Place chicken breasts, pocket side up, in the pan on medium heat and cook for 3 minutes. Continue to spray olive oil on chicken or in pan while cooking, as needed.
7. Using cooking tongs, turn chicken over and cook an additional 3 minutes on the pocket. Cook chicken a few more minutes on each side of the pocket, turning chicken with tongs to rotate. It is necessary to cook all four sides of the chicken.
8. Remove pan from heat and cover; let sit for 5 minutes to make sure center of chicken cooks through.
9. Any filling that may have spilled out may be placed on top for serving. Season with salt and pepper, to taste. Serve.

**Servings:** Entire recipe = 2 - 8 oz. lean protein + 4 C. veggies; ½ recipe = 1 - 8 oz. lean protein + 2 C. veggies

## BBQ CRANBERRY TURKEY MEATBALLS

**Ingredients:**
**16 oz. lean ground turkey or chicken**
**1 C. cauliflower florets**
**1 C. fresh mushrooms**
**1/3 C. liquid egg whites**
**1 tsp. garlic powder**
**½ tsp. IP salt**
**Other seasonings of choice**
**½ C. Walden Farms cranberry spread**
**½ C. Walden Farms BBQ sauce (or Rich & Sassy BBQ sauce, pg. 51)**
**Olive oil spray**

**Directions:**
1. Preheat oven to 350 degrees.
2. Place cauliflower and mushrooms

in a food processor; pulse to the consistency of rice.
3. In a large bowl, combine turkey or chicken, riced veggie mixture, garlic powder, salt, seasonings and liquid egg whites. Mix together gently until combined. Do not over mix or the meatballs will be tough.
4. Spray a baking sheet with olive oil cooking spray. Scoop meat mixture (about 2+ T. for each meatball) and gently roll portions between palms to form a smooth ball. Place on baking sheet.
5. Bake meatballs for 20 minutes. Remove meatballs from oven.
6. In a small bowl, combine the BBQ sauce and cranberry spread; heat 30 seconds in microwave on high. Stir to mix. Pour BBQ/cranberry mixture into a bowl and transfer meatballs to the bowl; toss to coat. Let the meatballs sit in the sauce; raise the oven temperature to 450 degrees.
7. Drain the moisture and wipe the grease from the baking sheet. Apply a fresh coat of olive oil cooking spray.
8. When oven has reached 450 degrees, give meatballs another toss in the bowl, transfer meatballs and sauce to the baking sheet and bake for an additional 15 - 20 minutes.
9. Top the meatballs with additional BBQ cranberry mixture (warmed), if desired.

**Servings:** Entire recipe = 16 oz. lean protein + 2 C. veggies; ½ recipe = 8 oz. lean protein + 1 C. veggies

## BRUSCHETTA CHICKEN
*A delicious family friendly recipe*

**Ingredients:**
**2 - 8 oz. chicken breasts, boneless and skinless**
**¾ tsp. sea salt**
**½ tsp. black pepper**
**¾ tsp. garlic powder**
**4 tsp. olive oil (divided)**
**¼ C. IP or Walden Farms balsamic dressing**

1 ½ tsp. minced garlic
4 C. cherry tomatoes or baby heirloom tomatoes
¼ C. chopped fresh basil

**Directions:**
1. Place chicken breasts in a large resealable plastic bag. Using a meat mallet, pound to ½ inch thickness; season both sides with salt, pepper and garlic powder.
2. Heat 2 tsp. olive oil in a large frying pan over medium/medium high heat; fry chicken breasts 3 minutes each side.
3. While chicken is cooking, heat the balsamic dressing to bubbling over medium/medium high heat in a small sauce pan. Turn down heat to medium/medium low; simmer 6 minutes, stirring occasionally. Set aside.
4. Remove cooked chicken from pan and cover to keep warm.
5. Add 2 tsp. olive oil, minced garlic, tomatoes and dressing to the hot frying pan.
6. Cover and cook over medium/medium low heat for 8 minutes or until tomatoes start to burst.
7. Plate chicken and top with tomato mixture; sprinkle with basil.

**Servings:** Entire recipe = 16 oz. lean protein + 2 C. veggies; ½ recipe = 8 oz. lean protein + 2 C. veggies

## BUFFALO CHICKEN MEATBALLS

**Ingredients:**
1 lb. ground chicken or turkey
2 C. (7 oz.) cauliflower florets
½ C. shredded zucchini
½ C. chopped green onions

1 tsp. garlic powder
1 tsp. onion powder
1 ¼ tsp. sea salt
1/3 C. liquid egg whites
Olive oil cooking spray
½ - 1 C. Buffalo wing hot sauce (sugar free), to taste
Walden Farms blue cheese dressing, for dipping
Celery sticks, optional

**Directions:**
1. Preheat oven to 350 degrees.
2. Place cauliflower, green onions and zucchini in a food processor; pulse to a consistency of rice.
3. In a large bowl, combine chicken (or turkey), riced veggie mixture, garlic powder, onion powder, sea salt and liquid egg whites. Mix together gently until combined. Do not over mix or the meatballs will be tough.
4. Spray a baking sheet with olive oil cooking spray. Scoop meat mixture (about 2+ T. for each meatball) and gently roll portions between palms to form a smooth ball. Place on baking sheet.
5. Bake meatballs for 20 minutes. Remove meatballs from oven.
6. Pour ¾ C. Buffalo wing sauce into a bowl and transfer meatballs to the bowl; toss to coat. Let the meatballs sit in the sauce; raise the oven temperature to 450 degrees.
7. Drain the moisture and wipe the grease from the baking sheet. Apply a fresh coat of olive oil cooking spray.
8. When oven has reached 450 degrees, give meatballs another toss in the bowl, transfer meatballs and sauce to the baking sheet and bake for an additional 15 - 20 minutes.
9. Top the meatballs with remaining Buffalo wing sauce, if desired; may be served with a side of celery sticks and Walden Farms blue cheese dressing for dipping.

**Servings:** Entire recipe = 16 oz. lean protein + 3 C. veggies; ½ recipe = 8 oz. lean protein + 1 ½ C. veggies

**TIP:** Celery is an unlimited veggie; however, I use the celery sticks to make up the remaining ½ C. of veggies necessary for the meal to equal 2 C. total per ½ recipe.

## CHICKEN CACCIATORE
*Crockpot Recipe*

**Ingredients:**
2 - 8 oz. frozen chicken breasts (boneless and skinless)
8 oz. canned Mexican style lime and cilantro tomatoes, undrained
2 tsp. minced garlic
½ C. chopped yellow bell pepper
½ C. chopped green bell pepper
½ C. sliced fresh mushrooms
1 ½ C. sliced zucchini (cut slices in half)
¼ C. chicken broth (fat free, low sodium)
½ tsp. IP salt
¼ tsp. black pepper
Greek seasoning, to taste (pg. 49)
2 tsp. olive oil

**Directions:**
1. In medium frying pan, heat olive oil on medium/medium high heat. When olive oil is hot, add mushrooms and zucchini; cook just until lightly browned.
2. Place the frozen chicken breasts into crockpot; add remaining ingredients making sure the chicken breasts are submerged in liquid. Sprinkle with Greek seasoning.
3. Cook on high for 4 hours.

**Servings:** Entire recipe = 16 oz. lean

protein + 4 C. veggies (1 C. of the veggie serving is tomatoes); ½ recipe = 8 oz. lean protein + 2 C. veggies (½ C. of the veggie serving is tomatoes).

**TIP:** If necessary to cook for 8 hours, cook on low heat. Cooking it for 4 hours on high makes the chicken melt in your mouth.

## CHICKEN AND MUSHROOMS WITH ASPARAGUS

**Ingredients:**
8 oz. chicken breast (boneless and skinless), cut into cubes
2 tsp. olive oil
1 C. sliced baby bella mushrooms
¼ C. chopped green onions
¾ C. fresh asparagus tips
½ lemon, juiced
2 T. fresh chopped parsley
Chicken broth (fat free, low sodium), as needed
Garlic powder, to taste
Onion powder, to taste
Salt and pepper, to taste

**Directions:**
1. Heat 1 tsp. olive oil in a nonstick frying pan over medium/medium high heat. Add cubed chicken; stir fry 5 minutes. Add chicken broth to pan as necessary to keep the pan from drying out; do this with the chicken broth throughout the dish. Remove chicken; place chicken on a plate and cover with aluminum foil to keep warm.
2. Add mushrooms and 1 tsp. olive oil to the pan and stir fry 3 - 4 minutes.
3. Add the asparagus, lemon juice, parsley, garlic powder, onion

powder, salt and pepper. Stir fry until asparagus is tender crisp.
4. Add chicken and green onions and heat through.

**Servings:** 8 oz. lean protein + 2 C. veggies

**TIP:** I cut the asparagus spear tips off the stalks and use the stalks to make Mockamole (pg. 50).

## CHICKEN & SPINACH PIZZA SKILLET

**Ingredients:**
2 T. olive oil
1 ½ lbs. chicken tenders
2 T. dried minced onion
14.5 oz. can diced tomatoes, undrained
¼ C. fat free chicken broth
1 tsp. salt
1 tsp. basil leaves
½ tsp. black pepper
½ tsp. garlic powder
½ tsp. oregano leaves
6 oz. baby spinach

**Directions:**
1. Heat oil in a large skillet on medium/medium high heat. Add chicken; cook both sides until browned approximately 8 – 10 minutes.
2. Add seasonings and dried onions halfway through cooking chicken.
3. Stir in tomatoes and chicken broth, continue to stir until the mixture comes to a low boil.
4. Reduce heat to low; cover and simmer 3 minutes until heated through.
5. Stir in spinach; cook 2 – 3 minutes or until spinach begins to wilt.

Season with additional salt and pepper, if necessary, to taste.

**Servings:** 1/3 recipe = 8 oz. lean protein + 2 C. veggies

## CHICKEN CAULIFLOWER FRIED RICE

**Ingredients:**
6 oz. chicken (cooked), cubed
1 ¾ C. (6.1 oz.) cauliflower florets, riced
¼ C. chopped green onion
1 - 2 tsp. olive oil
Garlic powder, to taste
2 - 3 T. chicken broth (fat free, low sodium)
1 egg, lightly beaten
Soy sauce, to taste
Black pepper

**Directions:**
1. Heat oil in a frying pan over medium/medium high heat. When the oil is hot, add the riced cauliflower. Stir fry approximately 7 minutes, or until lightly browned. Add the chicken broth 1 T. at a time to prevent the pan from getting dry.
2. Add the chopped green onion and garlic powder; stir fry 3 minutes or until the cauliflower rice is tender and lightly browned.
3. Pour beaten egg into the pan with the rice and stir fry until cooked, approximately 1 - 2 minutes.
4. Add chicken and heat through.
5. Serve with black pepper and soy sauce.

**Servings:** 8 oz. lean protein (6 oz. chicken + 2 oz. egg) + 2 C. veggies.

**TIP:** To rice cauliflower, add florets to

a food processor and pulse to get rice size bits. Cauliflower can also be riced using a hand grater.

# CHICKEN ZUCCHINI POPPERS

**Ingredients:**
**14 oz. ground chicken or turkey**
**1 C. grated zucchini, peel on**
**1 T. minced jalapeno pepper**
**1 egg, lightly beaten**
**¼ C. + 3T. minced green onion**
**3 T. chopped fresh cilantro**
**½ tsp. minced garlic**
**1 tsp. salt**
**¼ tsp. black pepper**
**¼ tsp. cumin**
**4 tsp. olive oil (for frying)**

**Directions:**
1. Microwave zucchini and jalapeno on high 1 minute. Press with a paper towel to absorb as much moisture as possible.
2. In a medium bowl, combine all ingredients except olive oil. Mix together just until incorporated.
3. Using hands, form oval shaped meatballs, making 12 poppers; set aside.
4. Heat the olive oil in a large fry pan over medium/medium high heat. When hot, add poppers.
5. Brown on all sides, approximately 6-7 minutes total; turn heat down to medium/low and cover. Cook another 8-10 minutes or until poppers are cooked through. Continue to turn poppers over as necessary during cooking to continue to cook/brown all sides evenly.
6. Season with additional salt and pepper before serving; eat with your fingers!

**Servings:** 12 poppers = 16 oz. lean protein + 1 ½ C. veggies; 6 poppers = 8 oz. lean protein + ¾ C. veggies

**TIP:** Dip poppers in a mixture of Walden Farms amazin' mayo mixed with a little Walden Farms raspberry dressing.

# CRAN-ORANGE CHICKEN BREAST

**Ingredients:** (chicken)
**2 - 8 oz. chicken breasts (boneless and skinless)**
**2 tsp. olive oil**
**½ tsp. IP salt**
**¼ tsp. black pepper**
**½ tsp. garlic powder**
**½ tsp. onion powder**
**½ tsp. dried oregano**
**½ tsp. Creole seasoning, sugar free**

**Ingredients:** (cran-orange sauce)
**2 T. Walden Farms cranberry spread**
**2 T. Walden Farms orange marmalade**
**½ tsp. soy sauce**
**¼ tsp. chili powder**
**¼ tsp. garlic powder**

**Directions:**
1. In a small bowl, mix together the seasonings; set aside.
2. Place chicken in a large resealable bag. Using meat mallet, pound to 1/2 inch thickness; season both sides of breasts with seasoning mixture.
3. Heat olive oil in a skillet on medium/medium high heat.
4. Place chicken breasts in hot skillet and cook 3 minutes on each side.
5. While chicken is cooking, place all ingredients for the cran-orange sauce in a small bowl; microwave 1 minute stirring halfway through cooking. Stir to mix.
6. Plate cooked chicken and drizzle with warmed cran-orange sauce.

**Servings:** Entire recipe = 16 oz. lean protein; ½ recipe = 8 oz. lean protein

# CROCKPOT BBQ PULLED CHICKEN

**Ingredients:**
**2 - 8 oz. frozen chicken breasts (boneless and skinless)**
**¼ C. chicken broth (fat free, low sodium)**
**2/3 C. Rich & Sassy BBQ Sauce, pg. 51 (or Walden Farms BBQ sauce)**
**Salt and pepper, to taste**

**Directions:**
1. Place frozen chicken breasts in crockpot, pour chicken broth over the meat and sprinkle with salt and pepper.
2. Cook on low 5 ½ - 6 hours; add BBQ sauce the last ½ hour to heat through.
3. Pull chicken apart using two forks, mixing it in with BBQ sauce.

**Servings:** Entire recipe = 16 oz. lean protein; ½ recipe = 8 oz. lean protein

**TIP:** For a variation, you may substitute Buffalo wing hot sauce (sugar free) for the BBQ sauce to make Buffalo pulled chicken.

# EASY OVEN CHICKEN FAJITAS

**Ingredients:**
**2 - 8 oz. chicken breasts (boneless and skinless)**
**2 tsp. olive oil**
**1 ½ C. sliced red bell pepper**
**1 ½ C. sliced green bell pepper**
**½ C. sliced green onions**
**Taco Seasoning (to taste), pg. 52**
**Juice of 1 lime**
**Cilantro, to taste**

**Directions:**
1. Preheat oven to 400 degrees.
2. Slice chicken breasts into 1" strips.

Place chicken strips, bell pepper slices and green onions into a large resealable bag; add olive oil and taco seasoning. Shake to coat.
3. Spread out in a 9" x 13" pan. Bake 35 - 40 minutes, stirring once halfway through baking process.
4. Squeeze juice from the lime over the top of the fajita mixture after baking. Sprinkle with cilantro.

**Servings:** Entire recipe = 16 oz. lean protein + 3 ½ C. veggies; ½ recipe = 8 oz. lean protein + 1 ¾ C. veggies.

**TIP:** Serve with Tortilla Wraps (pg. 34); make sure to count the veggie servings in the wraps.

# MAPLE DIJON CHICKEN

**Ingredients:**
16 oz. chicken thighs (boneless and skinless)
¼ C. Dijon mustard
¼ C. Walden Farms pancake syrup
¾ tsp. garlic powder
2 T. apple cider vinegar
Salt and pepper, to taste
Cooking spray

**Directions:**
1. Preheat oven to 450 degrees.
2. Place the mustard, pancake syrup, garlic powder and vinegar in a bowl. Mix.
3. Salt and pepper both sides of the chicken thighs; place in a sprayed baking dish large enough to accommodate the thighs.
4. Pour half of the mustard mixture over the thighs. Turn thighs over and pour remaining mixture over the top.
5. Bake 30-35 minutes or until a meat thermometer inserted in the thickest part of the chicken thigh reads 165 degrees.

**Servings:** Entire recipe = 16 oz. lean protein; ½ recipe = 8 oz. lean protein

# ORANGE CHICKEN
*This recipe submitted by Sarah Hansel*

**Ingredients:**
16 oz. chicken breast (diced), seasoned to your taste
1 T. olive oil (to brown chicken & then discard)
½ C. Walden Farms orange marmalade
½ C. Walden Farms BBQ sauce of your choice
2 T. low sodium soy sauce
1 T. minced dried onions or chopped green onions
2 cloves of garlic, minced
Crushed red pepper flakes, to taste (optional to kick it up)

**Directions:**
1. Brown diced seasoned chicken on stove top with 1 T. olive oil.
2. When browned and juices run clear, drain all liquid off.
3. Mix the orange marmalade, BBQ sauce, minced garlic, dried onions and soy sauce.
4. Pour over chicken and cook on low for 30 minutes.
5. Serve over riced cauliflower or steamed veggies.

**Servings:** Entire recipe = 16 oz. lean protein + 1/4 C. veggies (minced dried onion); 1/2 recipe = 8 oz. lean protein + 2 T. veggies.

**Crockpot Directions:**
This can be done in the crockpot using whole chicken breast as well. Cook seasoned breasts on low for 4 hours, drain off liquids and add the remaining ingredients. Cook on low an additional 30 minutes.

**TIP:** This is very good left over the next day, either warmed or eaten cold.

# OVEN BBQ CHICKEN

**Ingredients:**
16 oz. chicken thighs, boneless and skinless
Rich and Sassy BBQ sauce, pg. 51 (approximately 1/3 C.)
Salt and pepper, to taste
1 tsp. olive oil

**Directions:**
1. Preheat oven to 425 degrees.
2. Brush chicken thighs with olive oil; season with salt and pepper and place in an 8"x 8" baking pan.
3. Bake 20 minutes.
4. Remove pan from oven and brush chicken with BBQ sauce.
5. Place back in oven; bake 15 more minutes brushing the chicken with BBQ sauce halfway through baking.
6. Remove pan from oven and brush chicken with BBQ sauce. Let rest in pan 5 minutes before serving.

**Servings:** Entire recipe = 16 oz. lean protein; ½ recipe = 8 oz. lean protein

**TIP:** Excellent served over Cauliflower Mashed Fauxtatoes, pg. 90.

# PEANUT SATAY CHICKEN BREAST

**Ingredients:**
2 - 8 oz. chicken breasts (will require at least 2 hours to marinate)
2 tsp. olive oil
Marinade:
1 T. + 1 ½ tsp. Walden Farms peanut butter
¼ C. soy sauce

2 T. + 1 ½ tsp. lime juice
2 T. yellow curry powder
1 tsp. minced garlic
½ tsp. chili powder
1 ½ tsp. *peanut butter flavor extract (or add 1 more T. Walden Farms peanut butter)
1 ½ tsp. sugar free sweetener, granular

**Directions:**
1. Place chicken in a large resealable bag. Using meat mallet, pound to 1/2 inch thickness. Set aside.
2. To make the marinade, place all the ingredients in a medium size mixing bowl and whisk to mix; pour marinade onto the chicken breasts inside the bag. Seal the bag, releasing as much air out of the bag as possible. Marinate chicken breasts at least 2 hours in the refrigerator.
3. When ready to cook the chicken, spray or add 2 tsp. olive oil to a frying pan or grill pan and heat on medium/medium high heat. When the oil is hot, add chicken breasts to the pan and cook 3 minutes uncovered. Turn and cook 3 more minutes uncovered. When there are about 30 seconds of cooking time left, add a little marinade to the pan. Discard remaining marinade.

**Servings:** Entire recipe = 16 oz. lean protein; ½ recipe = 8 oz. lean protein

**TIP:** *You may purchase the peanut butter flavor extract at www.olivenation.com.

## SOUTHWEST CHICKEN NUGGETS

**Ingredients:**
8 oz. chicken breast (boneless and skinless)
½ packet IP Southwest cheese curls (crushed)
2 ½ T. liquid egg whites
Olive oil spray

**Directions:**
1. Preheat oven to 425 degrees.
2. Cut chicken breast into nugget size chunks; place in a medium bowl.
3. Pour egg whites over nuggets and mix to coat.
4. Press each nugget into the crushed southwest cheese curls, making sure to coat all sides.
5. Spray coat a baking sheet with olive oil; place nuggets on the baking sheet. Lightly spray the tops of the nuggets with olive oil.
6. Bake 4 - 5 minutes, turn nuggets and bake an additional 4 - 5 minutes or until golden brown and baked through.

**Servings:** 8 oz. lean protein + ½ restricted; the remaining 1/2 packet may be eaten as a snack.

## SWEET & SOUR CHICKEN

**Ingredients:**
16 oz. chicken breasts, cut in 1" cubes
Salt & pepper, to taste
1 T. olive oil
1/3 C. Sweet & Sour Sauce, pg. 52

**Directions:**
1. Season chicken with salt and pepper.
2. Heat oil in a medium size frying pan over medium/medium high heat.
3. Add chicken; stir fry for 10 minutes or until lightly browned.
4. Turn down heat to just under medium; add sweet & sour sauce, and stir fry an additional 4 minutes until sauce reduces and caramelizes.

**Servings:** Entire recipe = 16 oz. lean protein + 2 T. veggies (tomato paste in sauce); ½ recipe = 8 oz. + 1 T. veggies

**TIP:** Excellent served over cauliflower rice.

## TIKKA MASALA
*A popular Indian chicken dish full of flavor, spice and HEAT!*

**Ingredients:**
16 oz. chicken breasts, cut into ½" chunks
4 tsp. olive oil
½ C. chopped green onion
2 tsp. minced garlic
1 tsp. sea salt
½ tsp. black pepper
2 tsp. coriander
2 tsp. cumin
1 ½ tsp. paprika
½ tsp. cardamom
½ tsp. cayenne (optional, if you like heat)
¼ tsp. nutmeg
¼ tsp. ground ginger
¼ C. tomato paste
1 IP vanilla pre-made drink
½ C. chopped fresh cilantro

**Directions:**
1. Heat olive oil in a large skillet over medium/medium high heat.
2. Add onions, garlic and chicken; season with salt and pepper. Brown chicken approximately 10 minutes or until cooked through, stirring occasionally.
3. Add remaining seasonings; cook approximately 1-2 minutes to toast spices.
4. Turn down heat to medium/medium low. Add tomato paste and IP Vanilla pre-made drink to skillet; stir to mix thoroughly. Simmer and stir until sauce thickens.
5. Serve topped with cilantro.

**Servings:** Entire recipe = 16 oz. lean protein + 1 C. veggies (½ C. occasional + ½ C. select) + 1 unrestricted; ½ recipe = 8 oz. lean protein + ½ C. veggies (¼ C. occasional + ¼ C. select) + 1/2 unrestricted

**TIP:** Excellent served over cauliflower rice.

## TURKEY TACO LETTUCE WRAPS

**Ingredients:**
**16 oz. lean ground turkey**
**2 T. Taco Seasoning, pg. 52**
**1 tsp. onion powder**
**2 T. minced green or red bell pepper**
**¾ C. water**
**4 oz. canned tomato sauce (no added sugar)**
**8 large butter lettuce leaves**

**Directions:**
1. Season ground turkey with taco seasoning and brown in a skillet over medium/medium high heat.
2. Add the bell pepper, onion powder, water and tomato sauce; cover. Simmer on low 20 minutes or until tomato sauce is cooked down and liquid is gone, stirring occasionally.
3. Wash and dry lettuce leaves.

Divide the meat mixture equally among the 8 leaves. Roll into a wrap.
4. Serve with Pico de Gallo (pg. 50).

**Servings:** Entire recipe = 16 oz. lean protein; ½ recipe = 8oz. lean protein. Veggie count will be based on total consumption of bell pepper + tomato sauce + Pico de Gallo.

## TURKEY ZOODLE EGG BAKE

**Ingredients:**
**4 oz. lean ground turkey**
**2 C. spiralized zucchini (zoodles)**
**1 C. diced fresh tomatoes**
**2 T. chopped green onions**
**6 large eggs**
**1/3 C. + 3 T. liquid egg whites**
**4 tsp. olive oil**
**1 tsp. sea salt**
**½ tsp. black pepper**
**¼ tsp. nutmeg**
**Cooking spray**

**Directions:**
1. Preheat oven to 400 degrees.
2. In a small frying pan, brown the ground turkey; drain.
3. Spray a 10" x 10" casserole dish with cooking spray.
4. In a separate bowl, whisk the eggs and liquid egg whites with the oil, salt, pepper and nutmeg until blended.
5. Add the egg mixture to the casserole dish.
6. Add the zucchini noodles, tomatoes, green onions and cooked turkey to the dish and toss gently using tongs (or clean hands) until the zoodles are well coated and incorporated with the eggs. Distribute mixture evenly in casserole.

7. Bake for 25 - 30 minutes or until eggs are set and edges are golden brown.

**Servings:** Entire recipe = 16 oz. lean protein (4 oz. ground turkey + 12 oz. eggs mixture) + 3 C. veggies; ½ recipe = 8 oz. lean protein + 1 ½ C. veggies

## WHITE CHEDDAR CHICKEN FINGERS

**Ingredients:**
**8 oz. chicken breast (boneless and skinless)**
**1 IP white cheddar ridges**
**1/3 C. liquid egg whites**
**Salt and pepper, to taste**
**2 tsp. olive oil**

**Directions:**
1. Cut chicken breast into chicken finger size strips.
2. Place white cheddar ridges into a blender; pulse to crumbs. Spread out on a plate. Sprinkle with salt and pepper.
3. Pour egg whites into a shallow pan or medium size bowl; add chicken strips and toss to coat with the egg whites.
4. Roll one chicken strip at a time in white cheddar crumbs until coated. Set aside.
5. Heat olive oil in a frying pan on medium/medium high heat; add chicken strips to pan. Turn heat down to medium.
6. Cook 2 -3 minutes on each side or until crispy on the outside and cooked on the inside.

**Servings:** 8 oz. lean protein + 1 restricted

# Salads, Soups & Stews

Mason jar salads have become very popular as a convenient and time saving meal.

The anatomy of a make-ahead Mason Jar salad layered in the jar:

1. Dressing
2. Hard veggies – cauliflower, broccoli, cucumbers,
3. Soft veggies – tomatoes, green onions, etc.
4. Protein – eggs, lean meats such as turkey, ham, etc.
5. Greens – lettuce, spinach, arugula, etc.

Seal the jar with the lid, lasts about 1 week in the fridge.  Store right side up.

**Big Mack In A Bowl**
**Page 75**

**Jicama Sweet Pepper Slaw**
**Page 76**

**Nuttin' Honey Coleslaw**
**Page 76**

**Cauliflower Fauxtato**
**Salad - Page 75**

**Southwest Cheese Burger Salad**
**Page 77**

**Unstuffed Beef Cabbage Roll Soup**
**Page 80**

# Salad Recipes

## BALSAMIC & BASIL HEIRLOOM TOMATO SALAD

Ingredients:
2/3 C. Walden Farms or IP balsamic dressing
5 ½ C. Heirloom tomato wedges
½ C. thinly sliced red onion
2 T. chopped fresh basil, or to taste
¼ C. apple cider vinegar
4 tsp. extra virgin olive oil
2 tsp. sugar free sweetener, granular
1 tsp. salt

Directions:
1. Place the balsamic dressing in a small saucepan over medium/medium high heat. When mixture starts to bubble, reduce heat to low. Simmer approximately 8-10 minutes to reduce, stirring occasionally. Keep warm.
2. Place the tomato wedges and red onion in a large bowl.
3. In a small bowl, whisk together the vinegar, olive oil, sweetener and salt.
4. Pour the vinegar mix over the tomatoes, sprinkle with basil; fold gently to coat tomatoes.
5. Plate tomatoes; drizzle balsamic reduction over tomatoes.

Servings: Entire recipe = 6 C. veggies; 1/3 recipe = 2 C. veggies

TIP: This Heirloom tomato salad is delicious served over a plate of fresh spring lettuce mix. For another variation add cooled, prepared IP rotini pasta and add 1 unrestricted to the servings.

## BIG MACK IN A BOWL

Ingredients:
8 oz. lean ground beef
Salt and pepper, to taste
¼ C. chopped yellow onion
¼ C. chopped dill pickle (sugar free)
Shredded lettuce (unlimited)
2 T. Walden Farms thousand Island dressing

Directions:
l. Season the ground beef with salt and pepper; brown in a frying pan over medium heat. Drain off any fat; set aside.
2. Place desired amount of lettuce in a bowl; add browned ground beef, onion and chopped dill pickles.
3. Top with dressing and toss.

Servings: 1 - 8 oz lean protein + ½ C. veggies (lettuce is unlimited; no need to count it in the veggies servings)

## CAULIFLOWER FAUXTATO SALAD

Ingredients: (salad)
3 ¼ C. cauliflower florets, cut in bite size pieces
2/3 C. water
2 T. chopped red onion
¼ C. + 1 T. chopped celery
¼ C. + 1 T. chopped snow pea pods
2 hard boiled eggs, chopped or sliced (optional)

Ingredients: (dressing)
1/3 C. Walden Farms honey Dijon mayo
1 tsp. chopped chives (dry or fresh)
¼ tsp. lemon juice
½ tsp. Dijon mustard
¼ tsp. dried dill
¼ tsp. sea salt

1/8 tsp. black pepper
Paprika (for garnish)

Directions:
1. Place cauliflower and water in a medium bowl; cover with plastic wrap. Microwave 8-10 minutes on high or until fork tender (but not mushy). Drain in a colander and set aside.
2. Meanwhile, whisk together dressing ingredients in a small bowl. You will only be using 2 T. of the dressing to mix into the salad; reserve remaining dressing and refrigerate for another time.
3. In a large bowl, place all the salad ingredients except eggs; toss gently to mix. Add 2 T. dressing; fold into salad.
4. Add chopped eggs and fold, or slice and top the salad.
5. Sprinkle salad with paprika for color.

Servings: Entire recipe = 4 C. veggies + 4 oz. lean protein (if using egg); ½ recipe = 2 C. veggies + 2 oz. lean protein (if using egg)

## CAULIFLOWER TABOULI SALAD
### [Tabbouleh]

Ingredients:
3 C. cauliflower, riced (10.5 oz.)
¾ C. grape tomatoes, quartered
¼ C. chopped green onion
¼ C. chopped fresh parsley
2 T. chopped fresh mint
1/3 C. lemon juice
3 T. olive oil
2 T. soy sauce
Salt and pepper, to taste

Directions:
1. In a large bowl, gently toss

tomatoes, cauliflower rice, green onion, parsley and mint. Set aside.
2. In a medium bowl, whisk together the lemon juice, olive oil and soy sauce; pour over cauliflower mixture and fold to blend.
3. Season with salt and pepper, to taste.
4. Refrigerate.

**Servings:** Entire recipe = 4 C. veggies; ½ recipe = 2 C. veggies

## CHICKAMA SALAD

**Ingredients:**
**8 oz. cubed cooked chicken**
**¾ C. cubed jicama**
**2 T. Walden Farms mayo (any flavor)**
**¼ C. chopped green or yellow onion**
**¼ tsp. Creole seasoning**
**¼ tsp. smoked salt**
**1 packet IP sweet & salty trail mix**
**Lettuce, shredded (unlimited)**

**Directions:**
1. In a medium bowl, mix together all ingredients except lettuce.
2. Serve over shredded lettuce.

**Servings:** 8 oz. lean protein + 1 C. veggies + 1 unrestricted

**TIP:** As an alternative, you may eliminate the trail mix if you do not want to use an IP packet for this meal. You may also use alternative seasonings for the Creole seasoning and smoked salt.

## CLASSIC SPINACH SALAD

**Ingredients:**
**Fresh spinach, washed (unlimited)**
**Fresh mushrooms, sliced (unlimited)**
**¼ C. sliced red onions**
**2 hard boiled eggs, sliced or wedges**
**IP salt, to taste**
**2 T. Walden Farms honey Dijon dressing**

**Directions:**
1. Combine desired amounts of spinach and mushrooms in a bowl; add red onion slices.
2. Top with hard boiled egg slices or wedges.
3. Drizzle dressing over salad; salt to taste.

**Servings:** 4 oz. lean protein (eggs) + ¼ C. veggies (onions). The spinach and mushrooms are unlimited.

## CRUNCHY PEAR BALSAMIC SLAW

**Ingredients:**
**1 C. shredded green cabbage**
**¾ C. shredded red cabbage**
**¼ C. chopped green onion**
**¼ C. chopped cucumber**
**2 T. Walden Farms pear & white balsamic dressing**
**1 packet IP sweet & spicy trail mix or IP soy crisps (crushed)**
**IP salt, to taste**

**Directions:**
1. Toss the veggies with salad dressing and lightly salt, to taste.
2. Top with trail mix or crushed soy crisps.

**Servings:** 1 unrestricted + 2 C. veggies (cucumber is not counted and is unlimited)

## HAWAIIAN COLESLAW

**Ingredients:**
**½ C. shredded cabbage**
**¼ C. chopped yellow bell peppers**
**2 T. chopped green onions**
**1 T. Walden Farms honey Dijon dressing**
**1 T. IP mango pre-made drink**
**Salt and pepper, to taste**

**Directions:**
1. Place all ingredients in a bowl and mix together. Keep refrigerated until ready to serve.

**Servings:** ¾ C. + 2 T. veggies

## JICAMA SWEET PEPPER SLAW

**Ingredients:**
**2 C. jicama (cut the size of matchsticks)**
**1 C. julienned bell peppers (red, yellow and/or orange)**
**2 T. olive oil**
**1 T. apple cider vinegar**
**1 T. Walden Farms pancake syrup**
**1 T. minced red onion**
**½ tsp. garlic powder**
**¼ tsp. ground cumin**
**2 T. chopped fresh cilantro**
**Salt & pepper, to taste**

**Directions:**
1. Place the julienned jicama and bell pepper in a bowl. Set aside.
2. In a medium bowl, whisk the remaining ingredients.
3. Pour the dressing onto the slaw and toss to coat; keep refrigerated until use.

**Servings:** Entire recipe = 3 C. veggies

**TIP:** I eat 1 C. per day; there are 2 tsp. of olive oil per cup of jicama slaw, which is the daily protocol limit. You may reduce the olive oil in this recipe to 1 T. if you would like to eat 2 C. in one day, olive oil would be reduced to a total of 2 tsp. per 2 C. servings.

## NUTTIN' HONEY COLESLAW

**Ingredients:**
**1 ¼ C. shredded cabbage**
**¾ C. chopped tri-color mini sweet peppers (or bell peppers)**

1 packet IP sweet & spicy trail mix
2 oz. Walden Farms honey Dijon dressing
1 T. apple cider vinegar
¼ tsp. IP salt
½ tsp. sugar free sweetener, granular
½ tsp. herb seasoning blend of your choice

**Directions:**
1. Place cabbage and peppers in a medium bowl; set aside.
2. In a small bowl, mix together the honey Dijon dressing, vinegar, salt, sugar free sweetener and herb seasoning blend. Toss with cabbage mixture.
3. Add half the trail mix to the mixture; toss.
4. Plate the coleslaw; sprinkle with remaining trail mix.

**Servings:** 1 unrestricted + 2 C. veggies

## SOUTHWEST CHEESE BURGER SALAD

**Ingredients:**
8 oz. lean ground beef
1 package IP southwest cheese curls
Shredded lettuce (unlimited)
½ C. Pico de Gallo, pg. 50
Taco or Greek seasoning (to taste), pages 52 & 49
Walden Farms honey Dijon dressing

**Directions:**
1. In a medium skillet, brown ground

beef; season with taco or Greek seasoning, to taste. Drain any fat.
2. In a large salad bowl, layer lettuce, beef, southwest cheese curls and Pico de Gallo. Top with honey Dijon dressing.

**Servings:** 8 oz. lean protein + ½ C. veggies + 1 restricted (lettuce is unlimited and not included in veggie count)

## TACO SALAD

**Ingredients:**
8 oz. lean ground turkey or beef
1 T. Taco Seasoning pg. 52
1 tsp. diced jalapeno
Shredded lettuce (unlimited)
1 T. chopped green onion
Lime juice
1/3 C. Pico de Gallo Salsa, pg. 50
1 packet IP Dorados, any flavor (crushed)

**Directions:**
1. In a skillet over medium/medium high heat, brown ground turkey. Add taco seasoning and jalapeno during cooking.
2. Place lettuce on a plate, top with cooked ground turkey or beef and chopped green onion.
3. Drizzle with desired amount of lime juice.
4. Top with Pico de Gallo and crushed Dorados.

**Servings:** 8 oz. lean protein + 1/3 C. + 1 T. veggies + 1 unrestricted

## TUNA CURRIED ROTINI SALAD

**Ingredients:**
2 oz. albacore white tuna (packed in water, drained)
½ C. chopped yellow or red onion
½ C. chopped green pepper
½ C. chopped celery
½ C. chopped tomato
1 T. Walden Farms mayo (any flavor)
½ tsp. yellow curry powder

1 IP plain rotini, cooked and refrigerated until cold
Salt and black pepper, to taste

**Directions:**
1. Mix all ingredients together; serve cold.

**Servings:** 2 oz. lean protein + 2 C. veggies + 1 unrestricted

## ZESTY CUCUMBER SALAD

**Ingredients:**
3 T. white or apple cider vinegar
2 T. olive oil
1 tsp. sugar free sweetener, granular
3 medium cucumbers, peeled, seeds removed and diced
10 oz. grape tomatoes, diced
½ medium yellow onion, diced
1 T. chopped fresh dill or cilantro
Kosher salt, to taste
Freshly ground black pepper, to taste
½ tsp. crushed red pepper flakes (optional)

**Directions:**
1. In a large bowl, whisk together the vinegar, olive oil and sweetener.
2. Add cucumbers, tomatoes, onion, fresh herbs, salt, black pepper and red pepper flakes. Let marinate at room temperature for 20 minutes. Store in covered container in refrigerator.

**Servings:** Servings are based on how much Zesty Cucumber Salad is consumed; measure serving for veggie count. Cucumbers are unlimited; count onion & tomato.

# Soups & Stews Recipes

## BRAZILIAN SHRIMP STEW

Ingredients:
1 lb. cooked shrimp, tails off
½ C. chopped red bell pepper
½ C. chopped orange bell pepper
2 tsp. olive oil
¼ C. chopped green onion
1 tsp. minced garlic
1 can (14 oz.) tomatoes with green chilies (no sugar added)
2 oz. vegetable broth
2 T. lime juice

Directions:
1. Add olive oil to a large skillet and place over medium/medium high heat. Add red and orange peppers; sauté till slightly browned. Add green onions and garlic; cook an additional minute.
2. Add tomatoes and shrimp; heat through.
3. Add vegetable broth and lime juice; heat through.

Servings: Entire recipe = 16 oz. lean protein + 4 C. veggies; ½ recipe = 8 oz. lean protein + 2 C. veggies

TIP: Top with cilantro and hot sauce if desired.

## CHILI CON CARNE

Ingredients:
2 lbs. lean ground beef (may use turkey or chicken)
1 C. diced green bell pepper
6 cloves garlic, minced
IP salt, to taste
2 T. olive oil
¼ tsp. black pepper
3 T. cumin, or to taste
1 ½ T. chili powder, or to taste
28 oz. can crushed tomatoes, no added sugar

7 oz. can mild green chiles
1 C. sliced fresh mushrooms

Directions:
1. Heat a large skillet on medium high heat; add olive oil, garlic, mushrooms and green pepper. Stir fry until lightly browned. Add ground beef, brown; drain any fat.
2. Add the remaining ingredients, turn down heat and simmer for about 20 minutes.

Servings: Entire recipe = 32 oz. lean protein + 8 C. veggies; ¼ recipe = 8 oz. lean protein + 2 C. veggies

TIP: Divide the chili into 4 portions and refrigerate or freeze extra servings for another meal.

## CROCKPOT BEEF STOUP
### Beef Stew + Soup = Stoup

Ingredients:
2 lb. lean beef chuck roast
2 C. beef broth (fat free, low sodium)
3 C. water, divided
2 C. radishes, halved
3 C. sliced bok choy
3 C. sliced Portobello mushrooms
Garlic powder, to taste
2 tsp. olive oil
1 - 2 T. soy sauce, low sodium
Greek seasoning, (to taste), pg. 49
Cooking spray

Directions:
1. Spray crockpot with cooking spray (or use a liner); place chuck roast in crockpot. Add beef broth, 1 cup water, radishes, Greek seasoning and soy sauce.
2. Heat olive oil in a large skillet over medium/medium high heat. When hot, add bok choy and mushrooms,

sprinkle with garlic powder and sauté until lightly browned; add to crockpot.
3. Cook on high 6-7 hours; add up to 2 more cups water (or beef broth), as necessary, in the last 1 - 2 hours.

Servings: Entire recipe = 32 oz. lean protein + 8 C. veggies; ¼ recipe = 8 oz. lean protein + 2 C. vegetables.

TIP: I divide the stoup into 4 equal portions and refrigerate or freeze extra servings for another meal.

## GAZPACHO SOUP
*Served cold*

Ingredients:
1 - 28 oz. can plum tomatoes, juice included
2 T. tomato paste
¾ C. chopped yellow pepper
1 C. chopped zucchini, unpeeled
1 ¼ C. chopped English cucumber, unpeeled
3 T. + 1 tsp. extra virgin olive oil
1 T. apple cider vinegar
1 tsp. chopped garlic
1 tsp. sea salt
¼ tsp. black pepper

Garnish (optional):
Chopped fresh cilantro

Directions:
1. Place all ingredients (except garnish) in a blender or food processor; puree until smooth. You may need to do this in batches.
2. Chill at least 2 hours and keep stored in the refrigerator until ready to eat. Top with chopped cilantro, if desired.

Servings: Total recipe = approx. 5 C.

soup. After preparing, divide soup into 5 equal servings, those servings will count as 1 C. occasional veggies. Also 2 tsp. olive oil per 1 C. serving.

**TIP:** Served in a martini glass, this makes a nice presentation.

# GREEK ROTISSERIE CHICKEN SOUP
**With Roasted Vegetables**

**Ingredients:**
1 whole deli roasted rotisserie chicken, skinned
2 C. chicken broth or stock (fat free, low sodium)
1 T. Greek Seasoning, pg. 49
2 C. cauliflower florets
2 C. sliced cabbage
2 tsp. olive oil
Salt and pepper, to taste

**Directions:**
1. Preheat oven to 425 degrees.
2. Place rotisserie chicken in soup pot. Add chicken broth; add more broth if necessary to cover about ¾ of the chicken; sprinkle in the Greek seasoning. Simmer one hour, turning the chicken over once.
3. Meanwhile toss cauliflower and cabbage with olive oil, salt and pepper. Place on a baking sheet; spread evenly. Roast approximately 20 minutes or until browned, turning once during roasting.
4. Strip meat off chicken and return 12 oz. chicken meat to soup pot. Add roasted vegetables and more water and/or chicken broth as needed. Simmer 15 minutes on low heat. Season to taste with more Greek seasoning and/or salt.

**Servings:** Entire recipe = 16 oz. lean protein + 4 C. veggies (16 oz. raw lean protein = 12 oz. cooked); ½ recipe =

8 oz. lean protein + 2 C. veggies (8 oz. raw lean protein = 6 oz. cooked lean protein)

**TIP:** I use rotisserie chicken because it is easy; however, some rotisserie chicken is laden with fat injections, sugar rubs, etc.; you may ask the grocer for this information. An alternative method is to use 2 - 8oz. chicken breasts (boneless, skinless); put the raw chicken breasts in the soup pot and they will cook during the simmering process. Shred the chicken before adding the vegetables.

# ITALIAN WEDDING SOUP

**Ingredients:** (meatballs)
16 oz. lean ground chicken (or turkey or beef)
1/3 C. liquid egg whites
1 T. Sausage Seasoning, pg. 51

**Ingredients:** (soup)
8 C. chicken broth (low sodium and fat free)
1 tsp. dried basil leaves
2 tsp. garlic powder
1 tsp. kosher salt
¼ tsp. black pepper
1 C. chopped celery
¼ C. chopped green onion
2 ¾ C. fresh spinach leaves

**Directions:**
1. In a large bowl, mix meatball ingredients until combined. Refrigerate while preparing soup.
2. In a large soup pot, combine broth and seasonings. Bring to a boil over high heat.
3. Meanwhile, form approximately 22 meatballs. Using a small cookie scoop

is a perfect size.
4. Drop meatballs into boiling soup; add celery and onions. Turn heat down to medium high and simmer 25 minutes; stir occasionally.
5. Add fresh spinach and continue to cook 3-5 minutes or until wilted; serve hot.
6. Garnish with additional chopped fresh spinach (unlimited raw veggie), if desired.

**Servings:** Entire recipe = 16 oz. lean protein + 4 C. veggies; ½ recipe = 8 oz. lean protein + 2 C. veggies

**TIP:** Evenly divide soup into 2 servings; freeze or refrigerate additional serving for another meal.

# ROUX-LESS GUMBO
*This recipe submitted by Lauren Corcoran*

**Ingredients:**
1 C. (5.3 oz.) bell pepper, chopped
1 C. chopped green onion
1 C. chopped celery
1 T. minced garlic
1 - 2 T. olive oil
2 C. frozen or fresh cut okra
1 ½ C. tomatoes and chiles, canned
1 ½ C. petite diced tomatoes (no sugar added), canned
16 oz. diced chicken breast (or shrimp)
8 oz. lean turkey sausage or seasoned lean ham (no sugar added)
1 - 2 bay leaves
¼ - ½ tsp. dried thyme
1 tsp. gumbo file' (may omit if you cannot find this spice)
32 oz. chicken broth, or stock (fat free, may use low-sodium if you wish)
Hot sauce, to taste (if desired)

**Directions:**
1. In large pot, combine olive oil, bell pepper, green onions, celery, minced garlic and chicken. Cook over medium heat until vegetables are tender and chicken is done.
2. Once the above combination is cooked down, add diced tomatoes

and canned tomatoes and chiles.
3. Add chicken broth, seasoned meat (sausage or ham), bay leaves, thyme, file' and okra. Add enough water to cover ingredients; a little extra water will not hurt. It will cook down.
4. Bring pot to a boil; once boiling, reduce heat and simmer for 30 - 60 minutes, stirring occasionally.
5. When ready to serve, remove bay leaves.

**Servings:** Entire recipe = 24 oz. lean protein + 9 C. veggies; 1/3 recipe = 8 oz. lean protein + 3 C. veggies.

**TIP:** 3 C. canned tomatoes = 4 C. fresh tomatoes. Conversion for serving size has been calculated for you.

## TORTILLA SOUP
*This recipe submitted by Sarah Hansel*

**Ingredients:**
1 T. olive oil
½ C. green onions, finely chopped
3 garlic cloves, minced
1 C. yellow, orange or red sweet bell pepper, diced
1 C. zucchini or yellow squash, shredded
1 C. kale or spinach
1 T. diced jalapeno pepper (optional)
1 10-oz. can tomatoes and green chiles
4 C. low sodium, fat-free, MSG free chicken broth
1 lb. boneless, skinless chicken breast, cooked and diced
2 T. soy sauce
1 T. chili powder
2 tsp. cumin
Salt and pepper, to taste

**Directions:**
1. In a large saucepan, over medium heat, cook oil, garlic, onion, peppers, zucchini, kale and jalapenos until peppers soften.
2. Add canned tomatoes and chiles, chicken broth, cooked and diced chicken, soy sauce, chili powder, salt, pepper and cumin.
3. Reduce heat to medium/low and simmer 20 minutes.

**Servings:** Entire recipe = 16 oz. lean protein + 5 C. veggies; 1/2 recipe = 8 oz. lean protein + 2 1/2 C. veggies.

**TIP:** This recipe is very flexible. Use the vegetables leftover in your refrigerator. You may use beef sirloin or pork loin instead of chicken. If you like more heat, add hot sauce or crushed red pepper flakes. If you can't find the tomatoes and chiles in the same can, use 1 ¼ C. chopped tomatoes + ¼ C. green chiles.

## UNSTUFFED BEEF CABBAGE ROLL SOUP

**Ingredients:**
2 lbs. lean ground beef
4 ½ C. shredded cabbage
2 T. dried minced onions
2 (14.5 oz.) cans garlic fire roasted diced tomatoes, no added sugar (see tips below)
2 tsp. onion powder
1 tsp. minced garlic
2 tsp. IP salt, or to taste
1 tsp. black pepper
3 C. beef broth (fat free, low sodium)

**Directions:**
1. Heat a skillet over medium high heat; brown ground beef. Halfway through browning, add minced onion and onion powder. Drain any fat.
2. Place browned ground beef mixture in a soup pot or Dutch oven; add remaining ingredients and stir to mix.
3. Bring soup to a boil, cover and turn heat down. Simmer 30 minutes.
4. Adjust seasonings, to taste.

**Servings:** Entire recipe = 32 oz. lean protein + 8 C. veggies; ¼ recipe = 8 oz. lean protein + 2 C. veggies

**TIP:** I use fire roasted diced

tomatoes to add flavor; however, any flavor may be used. If using plain canned tomatoes, season the soup with additional herbs and spices, to taste.

## ZUPPA TOSCANA
**(Tuscan Soup)**

**Ingredients:**
1 1/2 lbs. lean ground pork (or turkey)
2 T. Sausage Seasoning, pg. 51
1/3 C. dried minced onions
7 C. chicken broth, fat free (divided)
3 C. kale, cut in bite size pieces
2 C. diced radishes
1 C. cauliflower florets, cut in bite size pieces

**Directions:**
1. In a large frying pan over medium/medium high heat, add pork, sausage seasoning and minced onion; cook until browned and done.
2. Meanwhile, add 2 C. chicken broth to a saucepan and bring to a boil. Add cauliflower florets, turn heat down to medium; simmer and cook until fork tender (approximately 15 minutes). Set aside to cool slightly.
3. Place the remaining 5 C. chicken stock, ground pork mixture, radishes and kale into a soup stock pot. Bring to a boil; cover and reduce heat, simmer 25 minutes.
4. Place the cauliflower and broth mixture in a blender; puree. Add to the soup and heat another 5 minutes stirring occasionally.

**Servings:** Entire recipe = 24 oz. lean protein + 6 C. veggies; 1/3 recipe = 8 oz. lean protein + 2 C. vegetables

**TIP:** Divide the soup into 3 portions and refrigerate or freeze extra servings for another meal.

# Snacks & Miscellaneous

Snacks can absolutely be included in a healthy meal plan; it just requires a little bit of thought and planning. Choosing a healthy snack can keep you full and satisfied. Researchers have found that those who snacked on nutritiously healthy foods felt full on fewer calories than those who snacked on nutritionally empty foods such as chips or cookies.

**Shiitake Bacon**
**Page 86**

**Bruschetta Flatbread**
**Page 82**

**Cauliflower Pizza Crust**
**Page 83**

**Caramel Apple Nachos**
**Page 82**

**Caramel Apple Jicama Stix**
**Page 83**

**Roasted Sweet Pepper Chili Bake**
**Page 85**

## BRUSCHETTA CRACKERS

**Ingredients:**
1 IP tomato basil soup mix (dry)
½ tsp. garlic powder
¼ tsp. IP salt
¼ tsp. Italian seasoning
¼ tsp. dried chives
Pinch of baking powder
1 tsp. olive oil
3 T. water
¼ tsp. crushed red pepper flakes (optional)
Cooking spray

**Directions:**
1. Preheat oven to 350 degrees.
2. In a medium bowl, mix together the dry ingredients thoroughly.
3. Add the liquid ingredients; stir to mix.
4. Line a baking sheet with parchment paper; spread batter very thin with a spatula or back of spoon sprayed with cooking spray (to prevent sticking.)
5. Bake 15 minutes. Remove from oven; cut in cracker size pieces with a pizza cutter. Flip pieces over and bake an additional 5 minutes or more.
6. Watch the crackers closely towards the end of cooking time since they will bake quickly.
7. Cool completely.

**Servings:** 1 unrestricted

## BRUSCHETTA FLATBREAD

**Ingredients:** (bruschetta topping)
½ C. IP or Walden Farms balsamic dressing
1 C. chopped fresh Roma tomatoes (clean out center of tomato; discard)
¾ tsp. minced garlic
3-4 leaves fresh basil, chopped
1 tsp. extra virgin olive oil
1/8 tsp. kosher salt
1/8 tsp. black pepper

**Ingredients:** (flatbread)
1 IP potato puree mix (dry)
¼ tsp. ground coriander
¼ tsp. dried oregano leaves
¼ tsp. crushed red pepper flakes
1 tsp. extra virgin olive oil
3 T. water

**Directions:**
1. Preheat oven to 350 degrees. (for flatbread)
2. In a small sauce pan, add balsamic dressing. Cook over medium high heat until mixture just starts to bubble.
3. Turn down heat to medium. Simmer 5-7 minutes or until dressing reduces and thickens; stir occasionally. Set aside to cool.
4. In a medium bowl, toss the re-maining bruschetta ingredients; set aside.
5. In a medium bowl, mix together flatbread dry ingredients.
6. Add liquid ingredients; stir to mix.
7. On a parchment lined baking

sheet, spread batter evenly in a 7" square.
8. Bake 10 minutes. Remove from oven and poke several holes in the crust; cut into four square pieces with a pizza cutter. Flip flatbread over and bake an additional 10 minutes; cool slightly.
9. Top the flatbread squares with bruschetta tomato mixture and drizzle with 1 – 2 T. balsamic dressing. Refrigerate remaining dressing for another meal.

**Servings:** 1 unrestricted
+ 1 C. veggies

## CARAMEL APPLE NACHOS
*With crispy cinnamon chips*

**Ingredients:**
1 IP crispy cereal mix (dry)
1 tsp. cinnamon
1 tsp. sugar free sweetener, granular
Pinch of baking powder
1 tsp. olive oil
3 T. water
Caramel Fried Apples, pg. 38 or
Zucchini Fried Apples, pg. 46
(for topping)

**Directions:**
1. Preheat oven to 325 degrees.
2. Place dry ingredients in a blender; blend to fine crumbs.
3. Pour crumb mixture into a medium bowl; add the liquid ingredients and stir well.
4. Line a cookie sheet with parchment paper; evenly spread

batter into a 7" diameter circle.

5. Bake 15 minutes, take out of the oven and cut into 6 wedges with a pizza cutter. Flip wedges over, turn oven off and bake another 5 minutes or until lightly browned.

6. Top with 'apples' and serve.

**Servings:** 1 unrestricted + add the total serving size amount of veggies used to top the crispy cinnamon chips.

## CARAMEL APPLE JICAMA STIX

**Ingredients:**
3 C. jicama stix (cut jicama the size of fries)
1 T. olive oil
1 T. + 2 tsp. apple cider vinegar
2 T. Walden Farms caramel syrup
1 T. Walden Farms pancake syrup
1 tsp. cinnamon
2 pinches salt

**Directions:**
1. Place jicama stix in a large bowl; set aside.
2. In a medium bowl, whisk the remaining ingredients.
3. Pour the caramel cinnamon mixture onto the stix and toss to coat; keep refrigerated.

**Servings:** Entire recipe = 3 C. veggies; 1/3 recipe = 1 C. veggies (there will be 1 tsp. olive oil per 1 C. serving)

**TIP:** Marinate stix in the refrigerator for 2-4 hours for best flavor; toss to coat before serving.

## CAULIFLOWER PIZZA CRUST
*Recipe for crust only; see TIP following recipe for pizza topping ideas*

**Ingredients:**
14 oz. riced cauliflower or 4 C. cauliflower florets, riced
1 C. water
1 tsp. Italian seasoning
1 tsp. garlic powder
½ tsp. crushed red pepper
1 large egg

**Directions:**
1. Preheat oven to 400 degrees.
2. Place cauliflower rice in a large microwave proof bowl; add water. Cover and cook on high 5 minutes.
3. Drain and cool in a large metal strainer.
4. In a small bowl, add remaining ingredients. Whisk to blend; set aside.
5. Place cooled cauliflower rice in a flour sack or tea towel; squeeze as much water as possible out until the rice is 'dry'. (Do not rush this step or the crust won't cook properly and will be too soggy; this procedure may take 3-4 minutes to squeeze all the water out.)
6. Place the cauliflower rice and egg mixture in a large bowl, and mix until well blended.
7. Line a baking sheet with parchment paper (not wax paper). Spread the cauliflower mixture evenly into a 7 ½" diameter circle.

8. Bake 30 minutes; flip and bake another 5 minutes. Cool on cooling rack and top with your favorite toppings.

**Servings:** Entire crust = 4 C. veggies + 2 oz. lean protein; ½ crust = 2 C. veggies + 1 oz. lean protein

**TIP:** The entire crust takes up all the veggies in one day for protocol (4 C.). You may choose to top with alternative sauces such as the Chimichurri (pg. 48) or Rich & Sassy BBQ Sauce (pg. 51) as a tomato based sauce will put you over in veggie count for the day. Or, top with the Spaghizza Sauce (pg. 51), add your favorite toppings and eat ½ the pizza; be sure to count the additional toppings toward your daily veggie and/or lean protein requirement. Pizza shown in picture features seasoned grilled filet mignon strips topped with a few slivers of red onion and cilantro; the base is Chimichurri sauce.

## CUCUMBER COINS
*A tangy, salty sweet unlimited snack*

**Ingredients:**
1 English cucumber
2 T. sugar free sweetener, granular
1 ½ tsp. ground coriander
1 tsp. kosher salt
¼ tsp. black pepper
¼ tsp. onion powder
3 T. apple cider vinegar
2 T. cold water

83

**Directions:**
1. Slice cucumber into ¼" coins; set aside.
2. In a small bowl, whisk remaining ingredients.
3. Place cucumber in a large resealable plastic bag and pour vinegar mixture over the top of cucumbers.
4. Store in refrigerator.

**\*Servings:** Unlimited; raw cucumbers are a free and unlimited snack. You will want to be mindful of the salt and sugar substitute intake when consuming.

# GYROS

**Ingredients:**
**1 lb. ground lamb (or ground chicken)**
**2 tsp. kosher salt**
**½ tsp. freshly ground black pepper**
**¼ C. chopped green onions**
**2 T. chopped fresh oregano leaves**
**½ tsp. minced garlic**
**1 egg, lightly beaten**
**Chicken Faux-caccia Bread, pg. 23**
**Tzatziki Sauce, pg. 52**

**Toppings:**
**Diced tomatoes, to taste**
**Diced yellow onion, to taste**

**Directions:**
1. In a medium bowl, combine ingredients with hands; (except toppings, Chicken Faux-caccia Bread and Tzatziki Sauce) mix until seasonings are evenly distributed. Cover and refrigerate for at least 1 hour or overnight.
2. Preheat oven to 300 degrees.

Place the lamb mixture in the bowl of a food processor. Process until a smooth puree is formed, 30 seconds to 1 minute, scraping down sides of bowl as necessary.
3. Line a rimmed baking sheet with aluminum foil. With moistened hands, shape the lamb mixture into a rectangle about 7" long and 4" wide. Bake 25 - 30 minutes or until the center of loaf reaches at least 155 degrees on an instant-read thermometer. Remove from oven and allow to rest for 15 minutes.
4. Adjust oven rack to highest position (1½ - 2 inches below broiler element) and preheat broiler. Slice the loaf of lamb meat crosswise into very thin 4" strips (about 1/8" thick; no more than ¼" thick). Lay the strips on a rimmed baking sheet lined with aluminum foil; broil until edges are browned and crispy, 2 - 4 minutes. Watch closely as the broiler works quickly.
5. Prepare the Chicken Faux-caccia Bread. Fill faux-caccia bread with 5 oz. gyro meat, ¼ C. Tzatziki Sauce, diced tomatoes and diced onions. Fold gyro sandwich and wrap one end with aluminum foil to serve.

**Servings:** Entire recipe = 18 oz. lean protein (16 oz. lamb + 2 oz. egg) + ¼ C. veggies (Measure amount of tomato and onion used to top sandwich and add to veggie count.) Also add 1 unrestricted if using the Chicken Faux-caccia bread wrap.

**TIP:** 8 oz. raw lean protein = 6 oz. cooked lean protein. Gyro meat is excellent on salads.

# HOMEMADE ESPRESSO
*Using a standard drip coffee maker*

**Ingredients:**
**8 T. (heaping) coffee grounds, any flavor**

**4 C. water**
**\* See tip regarding pre-made drinks**

**Directions:**
1. Pour water into standard drip coffee maker.
2. Add 8 heaping tablespoons coffee grounds to filter basket and brew.
3. Place coffee carafe in refrigerator to cool espresso.

**Servings:** 1 unrestricted

**TIP:** \*When espresso is cold, fill a shaker with 4 oz. espresso and add a pre-made drink. Shake; pour over ice. This is a great homemade version of a coffee house iced latte drink for a fraction of the cost.

# PERFECT PIZZA CRUST!

**Ingredients:**
**1 IP potato puree mix (dry)**
**½ tsp. garlic powder**
**¼ tsp. salt**
**¼ tsp. Italian seasoning**
**¼ tsp. onion powder**
**1 tsp. olive oil**
**3 T. water**
**¼ tsp. crushed red pepper flakes (optional)**
**Olive oil cooking spray**

**Directions:**
1. Preheat oven to 350 degrees.

2. In a medium bowl, mix together the dry ingredients.
3. Add liquid ingredients; stir to mix.
4. Spread batter evenly in a 7 " circle on a sprayed baking sheet with a spatula or back of spoon sprayed with cooking spray.
5. Bake 10 minutes. Remove from oven and poke several holes in the crust with a fork; flip crust over. Bake an additional 10 minutes.
6. Cool completely; this will allow the crust to become crispier.

**Servings:** 1 unrestricted (crust only)

**TIP:** Top with Spaghizza Marinara Sauce (pg. 51) or other sugar free pizza sauce. Add roasted veggies, sausage seasoned lean protein (recipe for Sausage Seasoning, pg. 51) or veggies and lean protein of choice.

# POUTINE
**A Canadian original dish**
(vegetarian style)

**Ingredients:**
1 recipe Best Gravy Ever, pg. 48
1 recipe Turnip, Jicama or Rutabaga Fries (recipes in veggie section)

**Directions:**
1. Make recipes according to directions.
2. Plate the fresh roasted veggie fries; pour gravy over top.

**Servings:** See recipes for serving sizes.

# PUMPKIN PIE OATMEAL

**Ingredients:**
1 IP maple oatmeal mix (dry)
½ tsp. vanilla extract
½ tsp. pumpkin pie spice
3 ½ oz. water
Cinnamon, to taste
Walden Farms pancake syrup

**Directions:**
1. In a small bowl, add vanilla, pumpkin pie spice and water to dry oatmeal mix.
2. Microwave according to directions on maple oatmeal package.
3. Sprinkle with cinnamon and drizzle with Walden Farms pancake syrup.

**Servings:** 1 unrestricted

# ROASTED GRAPE TOMATO ROTINI

**Ingredients:**
1 IP rotini
1 C. grape tomatoes, halved
½ C. diced English cucumber
½ C. diced red or green bell pepper
2 T. thinly sliced green onion
1 tsp. minced garlic
1 tsp. olive oil
IP Salt, to taste
Walden Farms or IP balsamic dressing, to taste

**Directions:**
1. Preheat oven to 375 degrees.
2. Cut tomatoes in half; place in a resealable bag with olive oil, salt and minced garlic.
3. Place halved tomatoes on a baking sheet and roast 20 - 22 minutes.
4. Meanwhile, cook rotini according to package directions.
5. Place cooked rotini, remaining ingredients and roasted tomatoes in a medium bowl.
6. Drizzle with Walden Farms or IP balsamic vinegar, to taste. Toss to coat. Serve.

**Servings:** 1 unrestricted + 2 C. veggies

**TIP:** This dish may be eaten hot or cold, makes a great meal for lunch.

# ROASTED SWEET PEPPER CHILI BAKE

**Ingredients:**
2 C. (8 - 10) tricolor mini sweet peppers
1 IP vegetable chili mix
1 egg, lightly beaten
Salt and pepper, to taste
Olive oil cooking spray

**Directions:**
1. Preheat oven to 425 degrees.
2. Prepare vegetable chili mix

according to package directions; set aside to cool.

3. Cut stem end off peppers, cut lengthwise and clean out seeds and membrane.

4. Spray coat a baking sheet with olive oil cooking spray; lay peppers, cut side up, on baking sheet and spray mist with cooking spray.

5. Roast 20 minutes.

6. Mix beaten egg into cooled chili mixture. Spray an individual size casserole dish with cooking spray; add chili mixture to casserole. Season with salt and pepper, to taste.

7. Layer roasted sweet peppers, cut side down, across the chili mixture to cover.

8. Bake 20 minutes or until egg is cooked through.

**Servings:** 1 restricted + 2 C. veggies + 2 oz. lean protein (egg)

## SHIITAKE BACON

**Ingredients:**
**2 C. shiitake mushrooms, thinly sliced**
**Olive oil cooking spray**
**Sea salt, to taste**

**Directions:**

1. Preheat oven to 375 degrees.

2. Coat a rimmed baking sheet with olive oil cooking spray.

3. Spread mushrooms in one layer over the entire baking sheet, spacing apart; spray coat the mushrooms with olive oil cooking spray.

4. Sprinkle lightly with salt; bake 25-30 minutes, turning with a spatula once during baking. Bake

mushrooms until they are dark brown and crispy but not burned.

**Servings:** 2 C. veggies

**TIP:** Baking time will vary depending on the thickness of the mushrooms, watch closely toward end of bake time or they will burn quickly. You may purchase the shiitake mushrooms pre-sliced in the produce section making this a quick, delicious and easy snack.

## TACO CHIPS

**Ingredients:**
**1 IP crispy cereal mix (dry), crushed**
**1 tsp. Taco Seasoning, pg. 52**
**Pinch of baking powder**
**1 tsp. olive oil**
**3 T. water**

**Directions:**

1. Preheat oven to 325 degrees.

2. In a medium bowl, mix together dry ingredients.

3. Add liquid ingredients; stir to mix.

4. Line a baking sheet with parchment paper; spread batter thinly and evenly making a circle.

5. Bake 15 minutes. Remove from oven and cut in wedges with a pizza cutter; flip pieces over, turn oven off and bake an additional 5 minutes or until lightly browned.

6. Cool completely. Serve with Mockamole (pg. 50).

**Servings:** 1 unrestricted

## ZESTY ITALIAN GARLIC CRACKERS

**Ingredients:**
**1 IP crispy cereal mix (dry), crushed**
**½ tsp. garlic powder**
**¼ tsp. salt**
**¼ tsp. Italian seasoning**
**¼ tsp. dried chives**
**Pinch of baking powder**
**1 tsp. olive oil**
**3 T. water**
**¼ tsp. crushed red pepper flakes (optional)**
**Cooking spray**

**Directions:**

1. Preheat oven to 350 degrees.

2. In a medium bowl, mix together the dry ingredients thoroughly.

3. Add the liquid ingredients; stir to mix.

4. Line a baking sheet with parchment paper; spread batter very thin in to a square with a spatula or back of spoon sprayed with cooking spray (to prevent sticking.)

5. Bake 15 minutes. Remove from oven; cut in cracker size pieces with a pizza cutter. Flip pieces over and bake an additional 5 minutes or more.

6. Watch the crackers closely towards the end of cooking time since they will bake quickly.

7. Cool completely.

**Servings:** 1 unrestricted

# Veggies

TIP:  Roasting veggies browns them nicely on the outside and sweetens their flavor in a way that even avowed veggie haters find hard not to like.  You may cut up the vegetables ahead of time so all you have to do is toss them with olive oil and seasonings and spread them on a baking sheet when ready to roast.  Always be sure to cut the veggies evenly in size so they roast at the same rate; spread them as far apart as possible allowing them to get nicely browned.

**Roasted Eggplant**
**Page 93**

**Okra Fries**
**Page 92**

**Roasted Radishes**
**Page 93**

**Roasted Smoked Brussels Sprouts**
**Page 94**

**Turnip Fries**
**Page 94**

**Zesty White Cheddar Fried Pickles**
**Page 95**

# Raw Veggie Weight Chart

| Size | Select Veggie | Grams | Ounces |
|------|---------------|-------|--------|
| 1 Cup | Asparagus | 134 | 4.7 |
| 1 Cup | Bean Sprouts | 100 | 4 |
| 1 Cup | Bell Peppers | 149 | 5.3 |
| 1 Cup | Broccoli | 91 | 3.2 |
| 1 Cup | Cabbage (all) | 89 | 3.1 |
| 1 Cup | Cauliflower | 100 | 3.5 |
| 1 Cup | Celery | 100 | 3.5 |
| 1 Cup | Chayote | 160 | 5.6 |
| 1 Cup | Collards | 36 | 1.27 |
| 1 Cup | Cucumber | 104 | 3.7 |
| 1 Cup | Fennel | 87 | 3.1 |
| 1 Cup | Green Onions | 100 | 3.5 |
| 1 Cup | Jicama | 130 | 4.59 |
| 1 Cup | Kale | 67 | 2.4 |
| 1 Cup | Kohlrabi | 135 | 4.76 |
| 1 Cup | Mushrooms | 96 | 3.4 |
| 1 Cup | Okra | 100 | 3.5 |
| 1 Cup | Onions | 160 | 5.6 |
| 1 Cup | Hot Peppers | 150 | 5.3 |
| 1 Cup | Radishes | 116 | 4.1 |
| 1 Cup | Rhubarb | 122 | 4.3 |
| 1 Cup | Sauerkraut | 142 | 5 |
| 1 Cup | Spinach | 30 | 1.1 |
| 1 Cup | Swiss Chard | 36 | 1.3 |
| 1 Cup | Turnip | 150 | 5.3 |
| 1 Cup | Yellow Squash | 124 | 4.4 |
| 1 Cup | Zucchini | 150 | 5.3 |

| Size | Occasional Veggie | Grams | Ounces |
|------|-------------------|-------|--------|
| 1 Cup | Beans (Green & Wax) | 150 | 5.3 |
| 1 Cup | Brussels Sprouts | 88 | 3.1 |
| 1 Cup | Eggplant | 82 | 2.9 |
| 1 Cup | Rutabaga | 140 | 4.9 |
| 1 Cup | Snow Peas | 98 | 3.5 |
| 1 Cup | Tomatoes | 180 | 6.3 |

## ASIAN GREEN BEANS

**Ingredients:**
2 C. fresh green beans
2 tsp. olive oil
1 tsp. chopped garlic
1/8 tsp. ground ginger
2 T. soy sauce
Water

**Directions:**
1. Steam the green beans by adding 1" inch water to a medium saucepan. Add the steamer basket; place green beans into the basket. Bring water to a boil over high heat. When water starts to boil, reduce heat to medium and cover. Steam approximately 8 - 10 minutes or until fork tender, checking occasionally.
2. In a frying pan, heat olive oil on medium/medium high heat. Add the garlic, ginger and soy sauce. Stir to mix.
3. Add the steamed green beans; sauté until heated through and slightly wilted.

**Servings:** 2 C. veggies

## BACON JICAMA HASH

**Ingredients:**
2 C. cubed jicama (1/2" cubes)
1 ½ C. sliced portobella mushrooms
½ C. chopped green onion
1 tsp. garlic powder
½ tsp. onion powder
2 tsp. olive oil, bacon flavored (or plain)
1 tsp. *bacon flavor extract, optional
Salt & pepper, to taste

**Directions:**
1. Place cubed jicama in a large bowl, and microwave on high 5 minutes.
2. Heat olive oil and bacon extract in a large skillet over medium/medium high heat.
3. Add jicama, garlic powder and onion powder. Fry, stirring occasionally, until browned. (This can take 25-30 minutes.)
4. Add mushrooms and green onion. Stir fry until mushrooms are browned

and cooked. Season with salt and pepper.

**Servings:** Entire recipe =
4 C. veggies; ½ recipe = 2 C. veggies

**TIP:** *The bacon flavor extract may be purchased from www.olivenation.com; it lends a salty smoky bacon flavor to the dish. This is a delicious side dish served with steak and eggs.

## BALSAMIC BRAISED RED CABBAGE

**Ingredients:**
2 C. sliced red cabbage
2 tsp. olive oil
1 tsp. sugar free sweetener, granular
1 T. + 2 tsp. IP or Walden Farms balsamic dressing
¼ C. chicken broth, fat free
Kosher salt, to taste
Pepper, to taste

**Directions:**
1. In a small bowl, mix the sweetener and balsamic dressing; set aside.
2. In a medium frying pan, heat the olive oil on medium/medium high heat. When oil is hot, add cabbage; sprinkle with salt and pepper. Stir fry 5 minutes.
3. Add balsamic mixture; stir fry an additional 3 minutes.
4. Turn down heat to medium/medium low and add chicken broth to cabbage. Cover and cook 3-5 minutes, stirring occasionally.

**Servings:** Entire recipe = 2 C. veggies (recipe may easily be doubled)

**TIP:** An excellent side dish, especially when served with pork.

## BUFFALO CAULIFLOWER POPCORN

**Ingredients:**
2 C. cauliflower florets, cut into bite-size chunks
1 tsp. olive oil
Seasonings of choice, to taste
Buffalo wing sauce (sugar free), to taste

**Directions:**
1. Preheat oven to 425 degrees.
2. Cut cauliflower into small chunks, about twice the size of a piece of popcorn as they will shrink. Try to keep them the same size so they roast evenly.
3. Place cauliflower chunks in a resealable bag with the olive oil and seasonings, to taste. (I often use a smoked salt blend and garlic powder.) The popcorn also tastes great with only sea salt and pepper.
4. Spread chunks on a baking sheet; roast at 425 degrees for 15 - 20 minutes or until crispy and browned. Flip chunks once during roasting.
5. Drizzle the roasted cauliflower with Buffalo wing hot sauce. Serve hot.

**Servings:** 2 C. veggies

## CAULIFLOWER ALFREDO SAUCE

**Ingredients:**
10.5 oz. (3 C.) cauliflower florets
1 tsp. minced garlic
¾ C. + 2 T. water
1 tsp. olive oil
Salt and pepper, to taste

**Directions:**
1. Cut cauliflower florets into chunks about the size of cherry tomatoes;

set aside.

2.  In a medium sauce pan, heat olive oil over medium heat; add minced garlic and cook until fragrant but not browned.

3.  Add the water and cauliflower florets to the sauce pan and bring to a boil.  (The water won't cover the cauliflower but that's okay.)  Once the water boils, reduce heat to medium/medium low; cover sauce pan and continue to simmer 8 - 10 minutes or until cauliflower is fork tender.

4.  Transfer the entire contents of the sauce pan into a blender or food processor.  Season with salt and pepper; blend until creamy smooth.  (Be careful with hot mixtures when blending; they can blow the top off a blender.  Place a towel over the lid and hold down while blending, or use a bullet style blender to eliminate this issue.)

**Servings:**  Entire recipe
= 3 C. veggies; 1/3 recipe
= 1 C. veggies

**TIP:**  The Alfredo sauce will need to be heavily seasoned to have flavor.  Use seasonings of choice; I recommend Cajun seasoning to bring flavor to the sauce.

## CAULIFLOWER FRIED RICE

**Ingredients:**
1 ¾ C. cauliflower florets, riced
¼ C. chopped green onions
2 tsp. olive oil
Garlic powder, to taste
2 - 3 T. chicken broth, fat free
1 egg, lightly beaten
Soy sauce, to taste
Black pepper, to taste
6 oz. cubed pork, chicken, steak or shrimp, cooked (optional)

**Directions:**
1.  Heat oil in a frying pan over medium/medium high heat.  When the oil is hot, add the riced cauliflower.  Stir fry approximately 7 minutes using the chicken broth 1 T. at a time, as needed, if the pan starts to get too dry.

2.  Add the chopped green onions

and garlic powder; stir fry and additional 3 minutes or until cauliflower rice is tender and done.

3.  Pour beaten egg into the pan with the cauliflower mixture; stir fry until egg is cooked, 1 - 2 minutes.

4.  Add cubed and cooked pork, chicken, steak or shrimp if desired.  Heat through.

5.  Serve with cracked black pepper and soy sauce, to taste.

**Servings:**  2 C. veggies + 2 oz. lean protein (egg) + other protein amounts if adding meats or seafood to the dish.

**TIP:**  To rice cauliflower, add florets to a food processor and pulse to rice consistency.

## CAULIFLOWER MASHED FAUX-TATOES

**Ingredients:**
14 oz. (4 C.) cauliflower florets
Garlic powder, to taste
Salt and pepper, to taste
Water or chicken broth, fat free

**Directions:**
1.  Cut cauliflower florets into chunks the size of a cherry tomato.

2.  Place the cauliflower in a medium sauce pan and cover with water or chicken broth.

3.  Bring to a boil; turn down heat and simmer 15 minutes or until fork tender.  Drain.

4.  Put the cauliflower on a large plate, and press down on it with paper towels to absorb as much moisture as possible.

5.  Place cauliflower in a food processor; add garlic powder, salt and pepper.  Puree.

**Servings:**  Entire recipe
= 4 C. veggies; ½ recipe = 2 C. veggies

**TIP:**  Fat free chicken broth may be substituted for the water to give the mashed faux-tatoes more flavor.

## CELERY ROOT HASH

**Ingredients:**
1 ½ C. cubed celery root
¼ C. chopped celery
¼ C. chopped green onion
2 tsp. bacon flavored olive oil (or plain)
½ tsp. smoked salt
1 tsp. Greek seasoning, pg. 49

**Directions:**
1. Place all ingredients in a large resealable baggie; shake to coat.

2. Heat a medium frying pan over medium/medium high heat; when hot, add hash mixture.

3. Cook uncovered, stirring occasionally, for 8 minutes; cover and cook an additional 8 minutes, stirring occasionally, or until browned and tender.

**Servings:**  2 C. veggies

**TIP:**  This recipe may easily be doubled, tripled or more – a very family friendly dish.  You may also use any flavor olive oil or choose to season with your own favorite seasonings in place of those listed above.

## COCONUT LIME CAULIFLOWER RICE
*Outstanding served with Blackened Grilled Mahi Mahi, pg. 56*

**Ingredients:**
14 oz. cauliflower florets, riced
2 ½ T. chopped green onion
½ lime, juiced
¼ C. chicken broth
¼ tsp. coconut extract
Salt and pepper, to taste
Olive oil cooking spray

**Directions:**
1. In a small bowl, mix together the chicken broth and coconut extract; set aside.

2. Heat a large skillet, sprayed generously with olive oil cooking spray, on medium/medium high heat.

3. Add riced cauliflower and green onion; stir fry approximately

10-15 minutes.
4. Add chicken broth mixture, lime juice, salt and pepper. Stir fry until heated through.

**Servings:** 4 C. veggies

## CRISPY RUTABAGA FRIES

**Ingredients:**
2 C. rutabaga, cut into fries
1 egg white
Salt and pepper, to taste
Chili powder, to taste
Garlic powder, to taste
Olive oil cooking spray

**Directions:**
1. Preheat oven to 425 degrees.
2. Place fries in a medium size bowl; add 1 inch water. Cover with plastic wrap and microwave 8 minutes on high.
3. Drain in a colander, pat dry and cool slightly. Set aside.
4. Meanwhile, place egg white in a small bowl and whisk about 30 seconds till frothy.
5. Place slightly cooled fries in a large resealable plastic bag, pour in egg whites and shake to coat.
6. Spray a baking sheet with cooking spray and place fries on sheet – spread them out so they are not touching each other.
7. Sprinkle with seasonings. Bake 18 – 20 minutes, flipping once halfway through baking time.

**Servings:** 2 C. veggies

**TIP:** You may easily double the recipe and will need 2 baking sheets.

## FLAWLESS KALE CHIPS

**Ingredients:**
4 C. kale

1 ½ tsp. olive oil (using spray mister)
1 tsp. garlic powder
½ tsp. onion powder
½ tsp. smoked paprika (use regular if you do not have smoked; optional)
¼ tsp. IP salt

**Directions:**
1. Preheat oven to 300 degrees.
2. Remove the stems from kale and tear leaves into large pieces by very quickly grabbing the base of the stem with one hand and pushing outwards along the stem to slide off the leaves.
3. Wash and completely dry the kale leaves - they need to be completely dry before baking or they will steam instead of getting crisp.
4. Spray mist the olive oil onto the kale chips and massage the leaves to get every nick and cranny covered. Place kale in a large resealable bag. Sprinkle with seasonings, close the bag and gently rotate the bag, letting the seasonings coat each piece.
5. Spread the kale leaves in a single layer on a baking sheet so they are not touching. Use two baking sheets if necessary. Bake 10 minutes, rotate the baking sheets and bake an additional 15 minutes, watching closely toward the end of baking time. (You do not need to flip the chips.)

**Servings:** 4 C. veggies

**TIP:** The chips will burn in a real hurry if they're not watched closely. Turn on the oven light and watch through the window; do not open oven door. When finished baking, place the chips on a cooling rack. As they cool, they will get crispier. Any stems left on the leaves are chewy and bitter; take care to clean the kale, it's worth it.

## GARLIC MASHED RUTABAGAS

**Ingredients:**
2 C. cubed rutabaga
1 C. chicken broth, fat free
Water
Garlic powder, to taste
Onion powder, to taste
Dried chives, to taste
1 T. milk

**Directions:**
1. Place cubed rutabaga in a medium-large sauce pan; add chicken broth and enough water to cover rutabaga.
2. Bring to a boil; turn down the heat slightly to a low boil. Continue to cook until rutabaga is fork tender, about 15 minutes.
3. Drain broth and remove excess liquid out of the rutabaga by placing on a baking sheet and blotting with paper towels.
4. Put rutabaga in a food processor; add seasonings and milk. Puree.

**Servings:** 2 C. vegetables

**TIP:** Turnips may be substituted for the rutabagas in this dish.

## GARLIC ROASTED TOMATOES

**Ingredients:**
2 C. fresh cherry or grape tomatoes
2 tsp. olive oil
2 tsp. minced garlic

**Directions:**
1. Preheat oven to 425 degrees.
2. Cut tomatoes in half. Place tomatoes, olive oil and garlic in a resealable bag and shake to coat.
3. Spread tomatoes on a baking sheet; bake 15 minutes. Flip tomatoes over and bake an additional 10 minutes.

**Servings:** 2 C. veggies

## JICAMA FRIES

**Ingredients:**
2 C. jicama, cut into fries
2 tsp. olive oil
Seasonings, to taste

**Directions:**
1. Preheat oven to 425 degrees.
2. Place jicama fries on a plate and microwave 3 minutes; blot with paper towels to absorb any moisture.
3. Put the fries in a resealable bag, and add the oil and sprinkle with seasonings of choice, to taste. Shake the bag to coat the fries.
4. Place on a baking sheet; spread fries so they are not touching.
5. Bake 25 minutes or until browned, flipping fries over once during baking.

**Servings:** 2 C. veggies

**TIP:** For seasonings, I like to use a chili lime or Cajun seasoning on the jicama fries.

## JICAMA WATER CHESTNUTS
### For Stir Fry

**Ingredients:**
1 jicama

**Directions:**
1. Peel jicama and slice to thickness of a water chestnut.
2. Lay each slice on a work surface and cut out small circles with a melon baller, also the size of a water chestnut.

**Servings:** Measure the amount of 'water chestnuts' before adding to dish to determine servings.

**TIP:** Do not throw away the scraps; dice the scraps and add to the stir fry recipe along with the Jicama Water Chestnuts.

## KOHLRABI HASHBROWNS

**Ingredients:**
4 C. shredded kohlrabi
1 T. olive oil, butter flavored (or plain)
½ tsp. onion powder

Smoked salt or sea salt, to taste
Black pepper, to taste

**Directions:**
1. In a large frying pan over medium/medium high heat, heat oil until hot.
2. Add shredded kohlrabi, season with onion powder, salt and pepper.
3. Fry, stirring occasionally until lightly browned and done, about 15 minutes.

**Servings:** Entire recipe = 4 C. veggies; ½ recipe = 2 C. veggies

## OKRA FRIES

**Ingredients:**
2 C. fresh whole okra
2 tsp. olive oil
Seasonings, to taste

**Directions:**
1. Preheat oven to 400 degrees.
2. Cut stem ends off okra; slice lengthwise in half.
3. Place okra in a resealable bag, drizzle with olive oil and season to taste. (I like to use smoked salt and a little cracked black pepper). Shake bag to evenly coat okra with the oil and seasonings.
4. Place okra, cut side down, on baking sheet; spread fries so they are not touching.
5. Bake 15 minutes; remove from oven and flip the okra, cut side up. Bake an additional 3 minutes to get crispy.

**Servings:** 2 C. veggies

## RADISH CHIPS
*Great for snacking*

**Ingredients:**
2 C. thinly sliced radishes (about 2 bunches)
2 tsp. olive oil
IP salt, to taste
Pepper, to taste

**Directions:**
1. Preheat oven to 375 degrees.
2. Wash and dry radishes; thinly slice radishes using a mandoline slicer.
3. Place radish slices in a resealable bag with olive oil and seasonings. Shake to coat radishes.
4. Place on a baking sheet; spread chips so they are not touching.
5. Roast for 15 minutes or until lightly browned. Cool.

**Servings:** 2 C. veggies

**TIP:** The thinner the slice, the crispier the chip. Watch them as they near the end of roasting time as they will burn quickly.

## ROASTED BROCCOLI

**Ingredients:**
4 C. bite size broccoli pieces
2 tsp. olive oil
Garlic powder, to taste
Salt, to taste
Lemon pepper, to taste

**Directions:**
1. Preheat oven to 425 degrees.
2. Cut broccoli into bite size pieces; place in a resealable bag with the olive oil and seasonings. Shake to coat broccoli.
3. Place on a baking sheet; spread broccoli pieces so they are not touching.
4. Roast 22 - 25 minutes or until lightly browned; flip once during roasting.

**Servings:** 4 C. veggies

**TIP:** After roasting, broccoli may be sprinkled with lemon juice if desired. Delicious added to soups.

# ROASTED CABBAGE
*Delicious added to soups*

**Ingredients:**
4 C. sliced cabbage
2 tsp. olive oil
1 tsp. garlic powder
½ tsp. IP salt
Other seasonings, to taste

**Directions:**
1. Preheat oven to 400 degrees.
2. Cut the cabbage into 2 inch strips. No need to be exact but strips should be fairly uniform in size.
3. Put cabbage in a resealable bag; add oil and seasonings and close bag. Shake and roll the baggie so cabbage is completely coated with oil and seasonings.
4. Place cabbage on a baking sheet; spread cabbage in a single layer.
5. Bake 20 minutes or until cabbage is golden brown.

**Servings:** 4 C. veggies

# ROASTED CHAYOTE SQUASH

**Ingredients:**
2 C. cubed chayote squash
Garlic powder, to taste
Salt, to taste (I use smoked salt)
Olive oil cooking spray

**Directions:**
1. Preheat oven to 425 degrees.
2. Cut the end off the chayote squash, peel off the skin with a potato peeler and cut squash in half. Remove center membrane area and cut squash in ½ inch cubes.
3. Lightly spray mist a baking sheet with olive oil cooking spray. Place cubed chayote on the baking sheet, spaced as far apart as possible; lightly

spray the chayote to coat.
4. Sprinkle with garlic powder and salt, to taste.
5. Roast for 20 minutes or until squash is browned; flip chayote once during roasting to get browned on both sides.

**Servings:** 2 C. veggies

# ROASTED EGGPLANT

**Ingredients:**
1 eggplant
IP salt
2 - 4 sprigs fresh rosemary or thyme
Garlic powder, to taste
2 tsp. olive oil

**Directions:**
1. Evenly cut eggplant in half lengthwise. Lay the eggplant halves cut side up on a work surface.
2. Crosshatch the eggplant in a diamond pattern by running a knife tip deeply and diagonally left to right down the eggplant about 4 times making sure not to cut through the skin. Repeat the pattern from right to left making a diamond pattern.
3. Press the eggplant open with your hand and sprinkle salt into the crevices. Let eggplant rest on work surface for 30 minutes.
4. Preheat oven to 400 degrees.
5. Pick the eggplant up and gently squeeze the water out of it. Wipe moisture off the surface with a paper towel.
6. Brush the surface with olive oil and sprinkle with garlic powder. Lay the herb sprigs on a baking sheet and place the eggplant halves on top of them, cut side down.
7. Roast 1 hour. The eggplant will collapse during roasting, remove from oven and let rest 20 minutes before serving.

**Servings:** 1 C. raw eggplant = 2.9 oz. Eggplants come in many sizes;

weigh the eggplant halves raw before roasting to figure out the serving size.

# ROASTED FENNEL AND RED CABBAGE SLAW

**Ingredients:**
1 C. sliced fresh fennel
1 C. sliced red cabbage
2 tsp. olive oil
Garlic powder, to taste
Salt, to taste

**Directions:**
1. Preheat oven to 375 degrees.
2. Slice the fennel and cabbage into strips keeping the size of the strips as uniform as possible.
3. Place fennel, cabbage and olive oil in a resealable bag; sprinkle with garlic powder and salt, to taste. Shake the bag to coat.
4. Spread veggies on a baking sheet.
5. Roast 20 minutes or until vegetables are wilted and showing bits of browning. Flip veggies once during roasting.

**Servings:** 2 C. veggies

# ROASTED RADISHES

**Ingredients:**
2 C. halved radishes
2 tsp. olive oil
Salt and pepper, to taste
Other seasonings of choice

**Directions:**
1. Preheat oven to 425 degrees.
2. Cut radishes in half or quarters, depending on the size of the radish; the larger radishes get quartered, the smaller get halved. Try to get them even in size so they cook at the same rate.
3. Place radishes and olive oil in a resealable bag; sprinkle with

seasonings, to taste.  Shake the bag to coat.
4.  Place on a baking sheet; spread radishes so they are not touching.
5.  Roast 20 minutes or until golden brown; flip radishes halfway through roasting.

**Servings:**  2 C. veggies

## ROASTED SMOKED BRUSSELS SPROUTS

**Ingredients:**
2 C. (6.2 oz.) Brussels sprouts, halved
2 tsp. olive oil
1 T. soy sauce
¼ tsp. garlic powder
¼ tsp. cumin
1 tsp. Walden Farms pancake syrup
1/8 tsp. cayenne pepper (optional)
Dash of liquid smoke

**Directions:**
1.  Preheat oven to 425 degrees.
2.  In a small bowl, mix together all ingredients, except Brussels sprouts.
3.  Put halved Brussels sprouts in a large resealable bag; pour marinade mixture into bag.  Gently turn bag several times to coat Brussels sprouts.
4.  Place Brussels sprouts, cut side down, on a baking sheet; discard any remaining marinade.
5.  Roast for 15 minutes; remove from oven and flip Brussels sprouts over, cut side up.  Continue roasting until desired doneness, approximately 5 - 10 additional minutes.

**Servings:**  Entire recipe = 2 C. veggies

**TIP:**  Brussels sprouts take on a nutty flavor the longer they are roasted.  I recommend roasting until deep brown in color.  The marinade is delicious on many assorted roasted veggies.

## SALTED CARAMEL CAULIFLOWER POPCORN

**Ingredients:**
2 C. (7 oz.) cauliflower florets

1 T. Walden Farms caramel syrup
2 tsp. olive oil
Salt, to taste

**Directions:**
1. Preheat oven to 425 degrees.
2. Cut cauliflower florets evenly in bite-size pieces a bit larger than a piece of popcorn (it will shrink when roasted.)
3. Place cauliflower in a resealable baggie; drizzle with olive oil and sprinkle lightly with salt.  Shake to coat.
4. Put cauliflower on a baking sheet; spread out.
5. Roast 20 – 25 minutes turning once during roasting.  Cauliflower should be crunchy and browned on the outside, tender on the inside.
6. In a small bowl, heat caramel syrup 15 seconds on high in the microwave.
7. Using a fork, dip cauliflower popcorn into the caramel syrup.

**Servings:**  2 C. veggies

**TIP:**  Dipping the cauliflower keeps the cauliflower crunchy like popcorn; drizzling or tossing the cauliflower with the caramel syrup will make the 'popcorn' soggy.

## TURNIP FRIES

**Ingredients:**
2 C. (10.6 oz.) turnips, cut into fries
½ tsp. garlic powder
½ tsp. onion powder
½ tsp. sea salt
¼ tsp. paprika
2 tsp. olive oil

**Directions:**
1.  Preheat oven to 425 degrees.

2.  Peel turnips and cut into fries; spread fries on a plate and microwave 3 minutes on high.  Blot with paper towels to absorb any moisture.
3.  Put the fries in a resealable bag, add the oil and seasonings.  Shake the bag to coat the fries.
4.  Place on a baking sheet; spread fries so they are not touching.
5.  Bake 20 - 25 minutes or until browned; flip fries over once during roasting.

**Servings:**  2 C. veggies

## VEGGIE KABOBS
*With Maple Garlic Soy Glaze*

**Ingredients:**
2 C. assorted bell peppers, cut in chunks
2 C. fresh whole mushrooms
2 C. (10.6 oz.) zucchini, cut in 1" slices
2 C. (8.8 oz.) yellow squash, cut in 1" slices
¼ C. olive oil
1/3 C. Walden Farms pancake syrup
1/3 C. soy sauce
1 tsp. minced garlic
1 tsp. apple cider vinegar
¼ tsp. black pepper

**Directions:**
1.  In a medium bowl, mix together olive oil, pancake syrup, soy sauce, garlic, vinegar and pepper.  Pour into a large resealable baggie; add veggies and turn several times to coat.  Refrigerate at least 4 hours or overnight.
2.  When ready to roast veggies, preheat oven to 425 degrees.
3.  Place veggies on skewers leaving at least ½" between them so they cook evenly.  Discard remaining marinade.
4.  Place kabobs on a baking sheet; roast for 25 minutes, flipping once during cooking.

**Servings:** Entire recipe =
8 C. veggies; ¼ recipe = 2 C. veggies

**TIP:** These may be cooked on the grill over medium/medium high heat until browned. Refrigerate leftover veggies.

## YELLOW SQUASH CHIPS
### (Summer Squash)

**Ingredients:**
**2 C. thinly sliced summer squash**
**Olive oil spray**
**Garlic powder, to taste**
**Salt and pepper, to taste (or other seasonings of choice)**

**Directions:**
1. Preheat oven to 200 degrees.
2. Using a mandolin on thin slice setting, slice squash the thickness of a quarter
3. Spray baking sheet(s) lightly with olive oil. Lay squash chips, untouching, on pan(s).
4. Lightly spray squash chips with olive oil. Sprinkle with seasonings.
5. Bake 2 hours or until golden brown.

**Servings:** 2 C. veggies

**TIP:** Watch closely towards the end of roasting time as the chips can burn quickly. Bake until golden brown and get them off the pan immediately to cool. Use a metal spatula to get them off the cookie sheet more easily. Do not use aluminum foil to line the pan as the chips will stick to it and be ruined. Done correctly, these chips are outstanding.

## ZESTY WHITE CHEDDAR FRIED PICKLES

**Ingredients:**
**Dill pickle slices or wedges**
**½ package IP southwest cheese curls**
**½ package IP white cheddar ridges**
**¼ tsp. salt**
**2 - 3 T. liquid egg whites**
**Olive oil cooking spray**

**Directions:**
1. Preheat oven to 400 degrees.
2. In a food processor, combine the southwest cheese curls, white cheddar ridges and salt; pulse to crumbs.
3. Blot pickles of excess moisture. Place pickle slices or wedges in liquid egg whites, coating thoroughly.
4. Press pickles into crushed crumb mixture, covering completely. Shake off excess crumbs.
5. Place pickles on a sprayed baking sheet.
6. Bake 10 minutes; flip pickles. Continue to bake an additional 10 minutes.

**Servings:** 1 restricted + veggies (measure amount of pickles before coating with crumbs to get the veggie count). Use remaining ½ packages for another meal.

**TIP:** Serve with an IP approved dipping sauce such as Walden Farms dressings, ketchup or dips.

## ZUCCHINI CHIPS

**Ingredients:**
**2 C. sliced zucchini**
**Olive oil spray**
**Seasoned salt (or other seasonings of your choice)**

**Directions:**
1. Preheat oven to 225 degrees. Line a baking sheet with parchment paper or nonstick foil and spray with olive oil. Set aside.
2. Slice zucchini into thin medallions, about the thickness of a quarter. (Either use a knife and a very steady hand or a mandoline slicer)
3. Lay slices on prepared baking sheet; spray lightly with additional olive oil cooking spray. Sprinkle with seasonings of your choice.
4. Place in preheated oven; bake 45 minutes. Rotate baking sheet and

bake an additional 30 - 50 minutes, or until chips are browned and crisped to your liking.

**Servings:** 2 C. veggies

**TIP:** These are best eaten within a couple hours of removing from oven, as they start to get chewy instead of crisp.

## ZUCCHINI NOODLES
### (Zoodles)

**Ingredients:**
**1 C. zucchini noodles (zoodles)**
**½ tsp. olive oil spray**
**¼ tsp. garlic powder (and/or seasonings of choice)**

**Directions:**
1. Cut off ends of zucchini; run the zucchini through a vegetable spiralizer.
2. Spray mist about ½ tsp. olive oil into a frying pan; heat on medium/medium high heat. Add zucchini noodles; sprinkle with garlic powder and/or seasonings of your choice.
3. Stir fry about one minute or until al dente. (Cooking too long will cause them to become limp and mushy).
4. Serve with your favorite sauce.

**Servings:** 1 C. veggies

**TIP:** To prevent the zoodles from becoming watery in a dish, salt the raw zoodles after spiralizing. Lay the zoodles on paper towels, place more paper towels on top, gently press down. Let rest 30 minutes. Remove top layer of paper towels and replace with dry paper towels. Roll zoodles up in the paper towels and gently press out remaining moisture. Stir fry according to directions above.

# Table of Contents by *Category*

# Table of Contents by Category

# Table of Contents by Category

# Table of Contents by JP Mixes

# Table of Contents by JP Mixes

# Table of Contents by JP Mixes

*Cooking Abbreviations and Measurement Conversions*

**Abbreviations**
C or c = cup
t or tsp = teaspoon
T or Tbsp = tablespoon
oz = ounce
lb = pound
pt = pint
qt = quart

**Conversions**
3 tsp = 1 Tbsp
2 Tbsp = 1oz or 1/8 C
4 Tbsp = 1/4 C
1 C = 8 oz.
2 C = 1 pt.
2 pt. = 1 qt.
4 qts = 1 gallon